FREE TEXT RETRIEVAL SYSTEMS

a review and evaluation

a report of the Free Text Retrieval Working Party
of the Inter-University Software Committee

Malcolm Bain, Richard Bland, Lou Burnard,
Jon Duke, Colin Edwards, David Lindsey,
Nicholas Rossiter and Peter Willett

TAYLOR GRAHAM

Published by
Taylor Graham
500 Chesham House
150 Regent Street
LONDON W1R 5FA
United Kingdom

Taylor Graham
Suite 187
12021 Wilshire Boulevard
LOS ANGELES
CA 90025
USA

ISBN 0 947568 42 5

Z
699
.A2
F73X
1989

Contents

List of Tables

List of Figures

Chapter 1

Preface

This book is the outcome of work done by the Free Text Retrieval
Working Party of the Inter-University Software Committee (IUSC). The
IUSC is, in effect, itself a subcommittee of the Inter-University
Computing Committee (IUCC). The IUCC was formed in the 1960s as a
medium whereby those concerned with academic computing in British
Universities could exchange ideas: the IUSC is a specialised offshoot
dealing with software issues. At any one time it has a number of
"Working Parties" which look at particular areas, and the Free Text
Working Party is one of these.

The present Working Party is the successor to an earlier group which was
a sub-committee of the Database Working Party. In its present form it
began work in February 1987. After early stages in which we clarified our
joint understandings about the nature of Free Text and its role in
academic research and administration, we have concentrated on the
evaluation of commercially-available packages for handling Free Text. For
reasons which are explained later, these are mainframe packages (although
some of them support microcomputer versions). This document is a
report on that evaluation.

The members of the Working Party are:

Dr Malcolm Bain   `CLSMB @St-And.SAVB`
    Computing Laboratory
    University of St Andrews
    North Haugh
    St Andrews
    Fife KY16 9SX
Richard Bland   `NBSCS @Stirling`
    Computing Science
    University of Stirling
    Stirling FK9 4LA
Lou Burnard   `Lou @Oxford.Vax`
    Computing Service
    University of Oxford
    13 Banbury Road
    Oxford OX2 6NN
Dr Jon Duke   `ECLDuke @Leeds.CMS1`
    Computing Service
    University of Leeds
    Leeds LS2 9JT
Colin Edwards   `Edwards @AFRC.ARCB`
    AFRC Computing Centre
    West Common
    Harpenden
    Herts AL5 2JE
Dr David Lindsey   `D.C.Lindsey @ABDN`
    Computer Centre
    University of Aberdeen
    Edward Wright Building
    Dunbar Street
    Aberdeen AB9 2TY
Nick Rossiter   `CL22 @Newcastle.MTS`
    Computer Laboratory
    University of Newcastle
    Newcastle NE1 7RU
Dr Peter Willett   `LI1PBW @Sheffield.PrimeA`
    Department of Information Studies
    University of Sheffield
    Sheffield S10 2TN

Anne Foord, then of Leeds Polytechnic, was a member of the Working Party in the first year of its activities. As we have moved towards a conclusion we have received very welcome help from Nigel Lodge of the Combined Higher Education Software Team, based at Bath University. Dr John Ashford, of Ashford Associates, kindly commented on an earlier draft of this report.

The Working Party was chaired by Richard Bland. The secretary is Peter Willett, with David Lindsey as first reserve. Lou Burnard contributed a Working Paper which has served as a framework for much of our work, and his energy and enthusiasm have been major influences on the Working Party. Malcolm Bain, Colin Edwards and Lou Burnard were each responsible for the evaluation of particular products, and all three cheerfully bore heavy burdens in consequence. Richard Bland acted as coordinator and editor of this document, to which all the members of the group have contributed.

The costs in terms of time and travel fell on our employers, apart from Richard Bland's travel costs, which were met by the Economic and Social Research Council. We are very grateful to the Universities of St Andrews, Oxford and Stirling and to the Agricultural and Food Research Council for the use of computer time. We also owe a great debt of gratitude to the suppliers of the three packages which we evaluated in detail. The three firms, BRS Europe, Harwell Computer Power and Information Dimensions, were unfailingly helpful and good-humoured throughout the exercise.

Chapter 2

Free Text

2.1 Introduction

The IUSC Free Text Working Party is concerned with software that is used to organise, store, retrieve and display large quantities of free text. Such software should also have some facilities for manipulating conventional data-types such as integer, real, logical and date, but these facilities need not extend to the manipulation of complex data structures of the type found in administrative data processing. Such requirements are well handled by formal database management systems often now employing the relational or CODASYL data models. Generally, however, such systems do not support free text searching of the type considered here particularly well. Free text software systems are characterized by comprehensive indexing mechanisms so that large texts (over 10Mb) can be rapidly searched for occurrences of particular strings. In systems where *word level* indexing is used, an index associates each distinct word occurrence with its exact position in a document; in other systems, the index may point less exactly to areas such as sentences, chapters or even whole documents. In the latter case, more exact searching (for example to find two words within a specified distance of each other) may require a second pass through a subset of documents identified by the index lookup, with consequent impact on performance and usability. Typical search criteria may include proximity matching, (i.e. retrievals for which the search terms must be located within a certain distance of each other or within the same sentence or paragraph), fuzzy or partial matching, (i.e. retrievals in which only a part of the search term is specified), and searching via an on-line thesaurus (a structured dictionary which, for a given word, returns information such as preferred term, broader term, narrower term and so on). Phrase searching (i.e. locating occurrences of terms containing more than a single word) is regarded as a special case of proximity matching, although it may be implemented differently. Free text systems typically employ a variable-length record structure, divided into a number of loosely organised components. We use the terminology "document" and "field" to refer to these levels; different systems use various different terms, and a system may (and ideally should) support more than two levels.

2.2   The role of Free Text software

We distinguish three main classes of user for this type of software: information providers, research groups and IT specialists, as defined below.

Information providers The requirement here is for large centrally-held information resources, to be used over lengthy periods of time by a wide variety of computationally unskilled end-users, perhaps via an information server or similar system. Applications often have an indefinite lifetime, longer than that of their hardware, and the institution is committed to the application as part of an IT strategy. Skilled resources will often be available to set up and maintain such systems. End-user interfaces must be robust, secure and easy to use. System interfaces must be powerful but need not be particularly simple, as skilled personnel will normally be involved in implementation. Such systems will also typically be fairly static in design. Performance and reliability are of great importance. Updating will usually be carried out by specialist (but not necessarily computationally-skilled) staff, distinct from end-users of the system. Typical applications: library catalogues (where existing off-the-peg software is felt to be inappropriate); specialist online databases such as law reports, text corpora etc.; centrally controlled office automation systems; University Senate and Council minutes and papers.

Individual researchers and research groups The requirement here is for smaller, personalised information resources, for use and development by individuals or groups of postgraduate researchers, either collectively or through some form of hierarchy. Both end-user and system interfaces must be equally flexible and powerful as well as being easy to use for the nonspecialist user. Robustness may be of lesser importance than for centrally maintained services, in that individual users will be willing to trade convenience of use for some such aspects. Ability to integrate systems with other software, for example user-written programs or conventional relational database systems is of greater importance. There may be a need for different and extended character sets in this work. Typical applications: as for other research database projects, but typified by large amounts of textual material which has to be analysed linguistically or which needs to be indexed in complex ways. It may also be useful to construct skeleton applications (e.g. for departmental bibliographic reference), which can be made generally available and customised for individuals within a department.

Information Technology specialists For teaching purposes and to provide 'state of the art' awareness for those teaching or researching current software practices. The scale of systems actually built may be modest, but it is important that a full range of features be represented, and that system interfaces are not so daunting as to preclude any useful experimental work in designing and implementing systems.

Because of the multiplicity of environments in which individuals from these three groups may find themselves, it is important that an applications package should run on a wide range of hardware.

2.3 The nature of Free Text

The need for specialised software to handle free text has to do with the nature of free text itself. Text has some obvious but far-reaching attributes which make it difficult to process in the same way as other forms of data, such as the numbers, alphabetic strings or bit strings which are the usual objects of data processing systems. Because sequences of text are usually of an indeterminate length ranging from a few hundred to many millions of bytes, specialised storage methods may be necessary. Text is composed of words and punctuation sequences, which may need to be stored and processed in different ways on different occasions. Even within words or punctuation sequences, it is common practice to use mark-up to indicate global processing options of various kinds.

Text is most unlike other types of data in the complexity of its structure. For the purposes of storage, as indicated above, a text may be regarded as a very long string. For analytic purposes however, substrings of the text must be identified. Often these substrings can be arranged into a hierarchic typology (e.g. document - section - paragraph - sentence - word); this is the model adopted by most commercially available software. Occasionally however, a structure needs to be defined which cuts across hierarchic divisions: verse lines and sentences in a narrative poem being one good example (a sentence may occupy more — or less — than one verse line). For research purposes it is often necessary to structure a text in a variety of complex ways: for example, to indicate the lineation of different versions of the same passage; to analyse a dramatic text in terms of acts, scenes, speeches, stage directions, passages attributed to one or more authors etc. The words of which a text is composed may be categorised in a variety of ways to provide continuous or discontinuous sequences within a text or text element. Sometimes linguistic or orthographic features of the words themselves are the object of attention (in stylistic or linguistic analysis for example); sometimes the entities or events described by the words are the primary focus of attention. Often both are important.

Although the data structuring capabilities of relational database systems are well adapted to support arbitrarily complex (but definable) structures, they provide few built-in tools for the analysis of text strings. The modelling process used in creating relational databases also leads to information structures which are not always appropriate to the types of analysis typically carried out on texts. Typical text analysis operations are described in Chapter A.8 below. Typical text processing structures (i.e. contexts) include

- the document
- the document set (a collection of documents identified by some search procedure)
- the context unit (that part of a document within which a given

search procedure is to be performed)

2.4 Functions of Free Text software

Functions typically supported by a good Free Text package may be grouped under the following eight headings:-

- definition and re-definition of text structures and contents
- retrieval of documents and document sets
- formatting and output of retrieved documents
- control and analysis of document terminology
- addition, deletion and modification of documents
- recovery from software and hardware failures
- control of access to data and facilities dependent on the status of the inquirer
- monitoring of database use and performance

A checklist of desirable features in each of these categories is given in Chapter 6 below.

Chapter 3

Overview of systems considered

The Working Party has in general confined itself to a consideration of software running on multi-user systems. This is in accord with present software technology. There are currently no distributed free text retrieval systems, and for the medium term future at least the provision of a textbase to a population of users is best handled by localising the data. Although there is a large number of products available for only single-user systems, we felt it to be important to look for products which could meet the range of requirements identified in Sections 2.2 and 2.4 above. In general, this confines the search to substantial (and expensive) software products which have been developed on mainframes and, latterly, on multi-user minicomputers. However, several of these have been successfully implemented on the larger microcomputers such as PCs with hard disk and expanded memory, and we return to this point later in this Section. We began by reviewing all systems which seemed remotely likely to fit the general criteria which have been mentioned above. In addition to considering all systems known to individual members of the Working Party, we also went systematically through directories of software in this area. This initial pass produced a "long list" of seven systems, which were:

- ASSASSIN; Associated Knowledge Systems;

- BASIS; Information Dimensions;

- BRS/Search; BRS Europe;

- CAIRS; Leatherhead Food Research Association;

- INFO-TEXT (subsequently replaced by INFO DB++); Doric Computer Systems;

- MIMER-IR; Savant Enterprises;

- STATUS; Harwell Computer Power.

All seven suppliers were contacted and sent a copy of a Working Paper. In some cases we experienced difficulty in obtaining a response from the suppliers, but the majority sent very full and helpful responses. After considering these responses we excluded ASSASSIN, INFO-TEXT and MIMER-IR from further consideration, and CAIRS was excluded after a site visit. An extended account of the reasons for excluding these four products forms Appendix C. It should be noted that each has, in its own way, considerable merit, and it should not be inferred that we regard them as defective from all points of view. The remaining three products are, then, BASIS, BRS/Search and STATUS. These three make up our short list, and it is these three which we have evaluated in detail.

The working party did not consider software running only on single-user systems in any detail. For those users described above as "information providers", at least, such systems were clearly inappropriate, while even for others, it was not clear to what extent adequate facilities were widely available. This situation is changing with the greater availability of high-capacity optical storage systems for micros, at which time the working party felt that a review would be more appropriate. It was noted that some mainframe systems were already available (sometimes only in cut-down form) for micros, sometimes with a much enhanced user interface. This was felt to be a highly desirable development. Even in the absence of large scale storage, micro-based systems were felt to be very useful for prototyping large applications (for information providers), for operating on subsets of large databases (for individual researchers) and for instructional purposes. In all three cases it was clearly important that the functionality of the micro and mainframe systems be identical.

Chapter 4

The Evaluation

In order to evaluate short-listed systems, a standard set of tasks was
developed as a benchmark. Four data sets were used:

- Approximately 117 electronic mail messages, with headers indicating
  sender, recipient and subject.

- A complete Shakespeare play, with overlapping structures: Act,
  Scene, Line ; Speaker ; Prose/Verse/Song.

- The six books of Homer's *Iliad* in the original Greek, in a
  nonstandard character set including accents.

- Text in complex user-defined format : a 500-record bibliographic
  tape in MARC format.

The full specification of these test data is contained in Chapter A.1,
below. Each system to be evaluated was mounted at a different site but
on broadly similar machines. BASIS was mounted on the Oxford
University Computing Service's cluster of VAX 8000s; BRS/Search on St
Andrews' University's VAX 11/785; STATUS on the AFRC's
VAX-11/785. All three machines are run under VMS 4. We are grateful
to the Directors of the three computing services for allowing us to use
their resources in this way. We should also like to acknowledge assistance
from Cranfield Institute of Technology in the assessment of STATUS. At

each site, the test data sets were loaded under the system being evaluated, and a large number of tests were made. The specifications of these tests are contained in the following sections, where they appear in parallel with our specifications for the desirable characteristics of a free-text package. Some of the details are relegated to Appendix A, which should be consulted by interested readers as required.

There are approximately 70 points in the text at which a specific question is asked about each package. These "questions" are in fact usually posed as instructions to the package evaluators and are shown in the text in italics. Each is followed by a set of responses, one from each evaluator. Results from these 70 "triggers" (our working term for them) are discussed in 15 summaries which appear at appropriate points in the text. Each summary notes the overall importance of the preceding features on a three-point scale of Very Important, Important and Useful. There is then an overall summary which forms Chapter 8. Internally, we used a scoring system based on weighted sums of the triggers to form the summaries, and then a weighted sum of the summaries to guide our overall conclusion. We do not show this working here to avoid any reader taking the actual arithmetic too literally — such a procedure, because of its inevitable crudity, cannot be a substitute for informed judgement.

Chapter 5

Interfaces

The following sections itemise the main considerations in user interfaces.

5.1 Command language

It is highly desirable that all functions should be available from a single integrated command language, analogous to SQL in relational database systems. *Comment on completeness and integration of "native" command language.*

BASIS Database creation and definition requires knowledge of a Data Definition Language (DDL); nearly all database manipulation facilities are accessible from the Basis Menu Language (BML); specialised reports are defined in a third language similar (but not identical) to BML. All three languages are simple for simple use, but rather old fashioned in flavour. DDL contains many redundant features and considerable functional overlap (e.g. field definitions require attention in several distinct places). BML is adequate for most simple purposes, but has no facilities for screen mode input beyond those required to drive a VT100 terminal. Report is a highly procedural 3GL. At Release L a new forms-based integrated interface from which databases may be designed without recourse to DDL, and a non- procedural report writer, will be available in addition to existing interfaces.

BRS/Search All user accessible executable programs start with the characters
BRS (eg BRSMAIN, BRSLOAD). Command options are consistent, help
on each command is available with the help option (eg BRSACCT -help).
The usual route into BRS/Search however is via the BRS command. This
offers a menu of secondary choices that depend on your privileges (users
with sufficiently high privilege levels may see options for database
maintenance, for example). One option invokes the native mode interface,
which is command-driven. It is also called the dot-dot interface since all
commands are prefaced by two periods. It can be called directly with the
BRSEARCH command. Another option invokes the Searchmate
menu-driven interface. It can be called directly with the BRSMATE
command. The Searchmate interface is used in the BRS/Search Primer
documentation, the Native mode interface is used in the User's Guide.
Two other options allow the use of two interfaces that can be used for
searching only (EAGLE and COLLEAGUE). A considerable amount of
context-sensitive help is available online in the menu-driven interfaces.
User authorisation and database definition is also performed through this
menu-driven interface, and is straightforward once you have a grasp of the
concepts and terminology. Thus database and thesaurus definition,
loading, searching/displaying and updating can all be carried out through
a consistent menu-driven interface. New interfaces and customised output
formats however require knowledge of MNS and Print-time formatting
commands respectively.

STATUS The command language allows you to carry out the various activities
related to SELECTing (and hence searching), CREATEing and
ENLARGEing a textbase. These three are seen as separate activities
within the database management function. Other utilities such as security
management are accessed separately, from the operating system. The
command language covers all necessary functions. In addition command
macros are a BASIC-like language used to perform functions such as
writing menus, performing global edits or adjusting screen messages.
They are recursive, may be chained together and are either textbase or
user specific. Macros are called as new local commands. To some extent
therefore STATUS can be made to mimic other, possibly more familiar,
query languages. Querying is a special command rather than a mode of
operation and requires a query terminator. STATUS IQ (see below)
allows natural language querying of a textbase.

Summary of Section 5.1 This is a **very important** feature of any
system; all three packages provide a more than acceptable interface
but BRS/Search scores by the very large amount of
context-sensitive help information that is available to the user, and
the consistent nature of the screen-based interfaces used for data
definition, validation, update and search.

5.2 Customised screens and menus

For some functions (e.g. online document retrieval, document modification, report generation) it should also be possible to replace this command language completely by customised screens or menus, as appropriate to an end-user. Customising of such screens etc. should be simple and flexible, and suitable very high-level languages (4GLs) should be available to assist in this task. *Create customised query screen as specified in Chapter A.2 below. Comment on ease of creation, power of tools (if any) and usability of result.*

BASIS Reasonably friendly front ends can be created using BML with comparative ease: examples are provided for the MARC and MAIL databases. User can position lines, blank screen, change some screen attributes, request and validate input etc. in BML profiles, which behave procedurally, (though they are in fact interpreted). BML syntax is simple, old fashioned, and difficult to debug, though a rudimentary built in line editor and tracing options are provided. The host operating system is always available if other programs are required from within a BML profile. For screen mode input, at present, forms must be defined in DDL. The user must explicitly specify line and column positions and screen attributes for each field and is unable to modify the way in which data is passed between the screen and the application. A screen painter is available at Release L.

BRS/Search Screen-based interfaces are well provided for in BRS/Search. An interpretative language called MNS (MeNu System) is available to write others. The supplied menu-driven interfaces (SEARCHMATE, EAGLE and COLLEAGUE) are all written in MNS themselves and are available in source form for inspection. A number of different types of terminals and microcomputer characteristics are pre-defined in standard text files, and new definitions can be added by users. An interface was quickly and crudely written in MNS for the evaluation, this allowed setting of the terminal type at the start and then offered a choice of the 4 test databases to search (or quit). If the MAIL database was selected you were then prompted for search strings in each of the defined fields (these could be left blank), subsequent options allowed you to merge (ie perform a hidden AND operation), and display retrieved information in brief and full forms.

STATUS SCREEN REVERT provides a full screen user interface which allows the use of formatted screens for composition of search queries of varying complexity including Boolean expressions (the question capture panel). It also provides single key choice of subsequent activities and a scrolled display mode in all four directions. At present there are five screens to choose from giving access to queries of varying complexity, and each user can by default access a particular screen in each textbase. The next release will allow customisation of the text provided on the screen. This feature is good on VT terminals, but of reduced value on PCs running Kermit as terminal emulator if the mapping of function keys has not been done so as to correspond to the screen options. Menus can be written in STATUS macros (see above), and an example was implemented with the trial textbases.

Summary of Section 5.2 All three packages allow users to customise the screens or menus to their particular application and there would seem to be little to choose between them for this **important** feature.

5.3   Communication with other software

5.3.1   Call-in

It should also be possible to access all functions of the software via system interfaces, so that user-written code can perform free text functions with minimal overheads. *Attempt to link user-written main program as specified in Chapter A.3 below. If successful, run the program. Comment on results.*

BASIS Most features of the package are accessible via a package of high-level Fortran-callable language interface modules. For a competent HLL programmer, this would be the recommended way to create good quality user interfaces. A Fortran program MMHLI.FOR was easily written for the evaluation to demonstrate use of the HLI. At release L an embedded query language facility is provided. This will enable BASIS query statements to be placed in a suitable language (e.g. Fortran, Cobol, C) and processed by a precompiler.

BRS/Search The 'engine' module of BRS/Search is available to programmers. The documentation on the 'engine' commands, and a guide to writing C programs in a VMS or UNIX environment to make use of these, exists (we have a copy), but is not a part of the normal documentation set. It is possible to link a user-written front-end to the appropriate BRS/Search object modules to achieve the same effect, (although these are not a part of the standard release). This is also possible under MS-DOS, VM/CMS and AOS/VS environments. All these tasks would rate as non-trivial. The documentation for host language interface will be available as standard at Release 5, however, most user interfacing is expected to be through MNS.

STATUS A user-written main program does not link to STATUS in the suggested manner, and there were no results from tests specified in

question three. However, there is an Application Program Interface for
STATUS which can be provided, but is not part of the standard STATUS
product. In this a program communicates with a STATUS sub-process via
Mailboxes, and this is demonstrable using Mumps programs, for example.

5.3.2 Call-out

It should be possible to extend both data input and report writing
facilities by use of standard operating system facilities (e.g. screen editors,
calling user-written code to perform statistical analysis etc.) *Attempt to
link user-written subprogram as specified in Chapter A.4 below. If
successful, run the program. Comment on results.*

BASIS A standard feature of the BML allows access to the host operating
system, by spawning a subprocess. In addition, there is a set of runtime
modules (known as BASLIB) which allows some sharing of data between
the BASIS system and user written code, (provided of course that the
latter can make sense of a Fortran COMMON block). This cannot
however be combined with use of the HLI routines.

BRS/Search Any available editor may be defined as the default editor for a
database. BRS/Search comes from the UNIX world, and is well-used to
spawning subprocesses. A subprocess may be spawned to execute
operating system commands, for example, and the simple test specified
could be carried out this way. As has been stated above, the standard
release of BRS/Search does not include object modules and so the test
results required could only be carried out through writing an interface (or
probably modifying an existing interface) with MNS. It is claimed that
because the MNS language is very rich this often eliminates the need for
this type of language call-out.

STATUS Possible via the STATUS CALL and SYSFILE commands to access
the operating system by spawning a sub-process. Not possible to access a
Fortran subroutine as required, but is possible via the Application
Program Interface (see above)

- Can output a text string from the operating system by e.g.
  `CALL WRITE SYS$OUTPUT "Hello"`

- Writing out a string of text for each retrieved record is possible
  using a macro but with considerable overhead in spawning.

- Writing out a string of text plus a data value for each record is not
  possible from standard STATUS in the required manner.

5.3.3 Integration with conventional DBMS

The ability to access both free text held in an Free Text system and conventional DP records held in a relational database system using a single consistent interface is highly desirable. Ideally, the end user should be unaware of any boundary between the two. *Comment on integration (if any) with RDBMS.*

BASIS In principle, any existing DBMS capable of using either of the two above interfaces could be integrated with BASIS, to some extent. It would not however be an easy task.

BRS/Search An application is in existence that maintains a BRS and RDBMS database in parallel. Again a non-trivial exercise.

STATUS In the VMS environment HCP have designed methods by which Oracle can call STATUS and vice versa. Prototype systems in which Oracle calls STATUS are in existence, and it is believed such an interface will be available in first quarter of 1989. In addition HCP say they are designing an SQL interface to STATUS which is due for release in the near future. Neither of these facilities have been evaluated.

Summary of Section 5.3 It is **important** that the package is not closed off and can interact with other software, e.g., user programs or another database package. The BASIS modules here are particularly successful in allowing user programs access to/from the system routines whereas the standard version of STATUS provides little assistance to the user in this respect.

Chapter 6

Functions checklist

This section discusses desirable facilities grouped according to the categories of Chapter 2.4.

6.1 Text Structure

6.1.1 Dictionary

Users should have control over and access to data dictionary or equivalent component, preferably using a simple flexible interface as proposed above. It should be possible for the user to determine the following information simply without leaving the interactive environment in which searches may be performed on a database:-

- The names and indexing characteristics of all items that can be searched in the current database

- The names and definitions of any pre-defined commands, macro procedures, input screens, reports etc. available

For each test data set, attempt to carry out procedures specified in Appendix A.5 below. Comment on results.

BASIS When existing documents are unaffected, adding a new field or changing the characteristics of an existing one requires: (a) add information to the DDL file defining the new field and its indexing features (b) recompile the DDL. This applies to all the changes specified above. When existing documents are affected by the change, a number of options are available. Macro procedures to insert default or calculated values for new fields can be defined using BML or any other interface. If existing data is to be re-indexed, the IFMGR utility can be used to unload and reload the affected fields only. Data is not changed in the index in-situ; the headfile is not affected. Changes in validation rules can be applied retrospectively, at the cost of re-processing all existing records. This can usually be done simply, by using the built in line editor.

BRS/Search When existing documents are unaffected only the database form file needs to be modified and reloaded. If existing documents are affected then the only safe thing to do is reload the database files. The BRSLOAD utility can do this.

STATUS To add a new field to a textbase : A keyed field can be added at any time, as long as +SPARE spare concorded named sections have been specified at time of textbase creation; the utility STSECMOD then allows these to be used later. To define about 20% extra such sections is recommended. These do not affect exisiting documents. Any new non-concorded named sections can be added at any time. There is no need to reconstruct the textbase in either circumstance. To insert a default value for the new field in existing documents or to derive a value in existing documents the existing textbase data must be globally edited using macros and the STATUS line editor, and the changes submitted to the amendment list.

To change a field definition :

- a keyed field name can be changed by globally editing the relevant records and submitting the changes to the amendment list. A named section field name could be changed by introducing the new name through one of the +SPARE fields and globally editing existing data as for a keyed field. No field name synonyms available

- Field lengths need not be increased since they have no defined length.

- Field lengths need not be decreased since they have no defined length.

- Changing of data types applies only to keyed fields. Use a new keyed field of the required type and globally edit existing data.

- Concorded named sections cannot be unconcorded or vice versa - the textbase must be recreated.

- No value validation rules can be imposed and therefore they can not be changed after textbase construction.

- Thesaurus control is available only at search time and therefore changing the method of thesaurus control of terminology has no meaning.

6.1.2 Datatypes

Full range of conventional datatypes should be supported (int, real, char*n, logical, time, date). It should be possible to extend the range of datatypes supported by the use of abstract datatypes. Support for multiple character sets is also highly desirable. *Note which of these supported. Note whether facilities exist for user-defined types and whether these can be specified as ADTs.*

BASIS Datatypes supported are integer, real (to specified precision), date, time, fixed length string, string, or long text. No support for abstract datatypes. Alternate character sets may be specified (database wide) in a dialogue file; the large variety of indexing facilities may also be relevant here.

BRS/Search Character, short-integer, long-integer, fixed decimal, single- and double- precision floating point are supported. Date supported in numeric form only. Alternate character sets may be defined, thus foreign language databases can be built and searched. No abstract data types can be defined.

STATUS The following are supported - characters, real numbers, integers, logicals (indirectly), and date in two formats. No abstract datatypes can be defined. Date and numerical datatypes are only of significance if defined as keyed fields. STATUS is distributed with Scandinavian, German, and French character sets. Others may be created by changing a single table.

6.1.3 Indexing

Multiple indexing is essential. It should be possible to index different parts of a document in different ways, to index the same part of a document in more than one way, or not to index them at all. *Carry out test specified in Appendix A.6, below, and comment on results.*

BASIS Phrase searching as such is not supported by means of an index but by use of proximity matching features in the command language. The MAP facility is used to define multi-field indexing capability: e.g. to search all the NOTE fields in the MARCdatabase independently or together, to search topic and message fields in the MAIL database independently or together. Accent blind or sensitive searching may be supported (as in the HOMER database) by using an additional index prefix. Categorisation of the text in the Shakespeare play (verse, prose etc) was achieved in a similar way. For example, to find all Armado's prose speeches in acts 1 to 3 containing the word "Honour" one might use

find prose=honour and speaker=armado and act le 3

A similar mechanism could be used to distinguish italic and non-italic text, but to support this as well as the prose/verse distinction would not be as easy, since context units may not overlap. It would however be possible at the expense of considerable preprocessing of the index transactions. It should be noted that the methods used in both the Shakespeare and Homer testcases depend on access to the index transactions file. As there are major changes in the way this file is used at Release L it is possible that different tactics would be more appropriate in future versions of the software.

BRS/Search By default, all fields are searched. Phrase searching (eg in the MARC database) is supported by the word proximity facilities. Individual fields may however be searched. For convenience in searching and display, groups of fields may be given an equivalence name, eg BRF: FROM, DATE, SUBJ in the mail database. Also in the mail database, date searching is supported in numeric form only, but dates are displayed in alphanumeric form for enhanced readability. In the Homer database accent blind/sensitive requirements are supported by implementing 2 databases. In Release 5 of BRS/Search it should be possible to search both simultaneously. In the Shakespeare database, the simple structure imposed on the data enabled a requirement such as, "recover all prose speeches of Armado in which the word honour appears" to be attempted with the search

"armado>" same "prose>" same honour

This indeed finds the required speech, but could find other, spurious, entries in theory. Act, Scene and Line Number searches could have been supported if implemented in the test, as could searching for special characters (cf Homer). Because the input text was essentially unedited, the default output is easily recognisable.

STATUS One index allows both phrase and word searching since word positions are maintained in the concordance. In the MARC data which was used to demonstrate this the keywords and titles are different named

sections and therefore distinguishable. For the electronic mail messages indexes were built on senders, value of date and on contents of topic and message fields. They were all part of the same concordance but could be distinguished by section name. The topic and the message text could be searched for independently, or together by naming both sections :
Word @ (SUBJECT,MESSAGE)
or through a macro which combined both sections. However, it was not possible to declare characters as accents or to identify characters to be optionally ignored. Accent blind searching is therefore not possible in the same textbase except by declaring all accented versions as synonyms. When using separate textbases it was necessary to know the probable position of accents to allow for their possible presence by leaving spaces in the search terms, ie the accent characters were treated as terminators. Where accent characters were included it was necessary to surround these characters in single quotes for searching or to trap their entry in macros. The searching of the Shakespeare text is controlled by the imposed structure rather than by indexing strategies. Search can be restricted to particular acts by the CHAPTER command and scenes within this isolated by browsing commands or by the A type keyed fields. Line numbers are a search term like any other text string. Text strings spoken by individuals are labelled as named sections, and specification of text type are kept as part of normal text. Using this structure the example search can not be achieved, but could have been possible had further text marking been imposed. This would have added the text type to the beginning of each speech where it does not now occur and paragraph markers at any change of text type during the same speech. The query
Q HONOUR//PROSE @ ARMADO ?
would retrieve the relevant text. Where speech types cross speaker changes it is not possible to retrieve words co-occurring in that same verse (for example). The CONTEXT and ZOOM commands are particularly useful in both the Homer and Shakespeare TEXTBASES.

6.1.4   Hierarchies

Hierarchic structures should always be definable (e.g. document contains paragraphs contains sentences). Non hierarchic structures (e.g sentences within verse lines, or paragraphs split across page boundaries) are also desirable. *Comment on results of attempt to mount Shakespeare data.*

BASIS Basic structural unit is document: cross-document searching is not possible. A document is hierarchically divided into fields, fields into elements, elements into sub-elements. However, there may be more than one hierarchy of elements and sub-elements within a given field, because different indexing prefixes may be applied to parts of the same field. Links between elements of different fields may also be established: this was used in the Shakespeare data. In this dataset, verse/prose codes in the TTYPE field can be linked with the context units into which the SPEECH field is subdivided, in much the same way as the line-numbers in the LINES field are associated with verse lines. The indexing prefix for parts of the text is modified to VERSE, PROSE or STAGE to indicate its type independently of these structural flags. Repeated occurrences of the same field are not supported currently but will be at Release L.

BRS/Search The basic structure of a BRS database is: Database - Document - Paragraph (or field) - Subparagraph (a typical paragraph in prose) - Sentence - Word. Cross database searching is not generally possible, although 'saved' searches may be applied to a number of databases consecutively. This facility is offered in the Searchmate interface, and in the next release of BRS (Release 5) it will be possible to search up to 16 databases simultaneously. For numerical data only, a paragraph may have a further division (eg LENGTH, WIDTH, HEIGHT within a paragraph DIMENSION). In general however, hierarchies within paragraphs are not possible, thus mounting the Shakespeare data to achieve easily all the searches desired, is problematical. (See Appendix A.1 for further information). A field (paragraph) may be repeated up to 65,000 times to create subparagraphs.

STATUS The basic retrieval unit is an article. These can be organised into a series of chapters. Articles are divided into STATUS paragraphs, named sections (fields) and keyed fields. Paragraphs start where marked or at start of named section. The user is asked to state the maximum number of words in a paragraph, paragraphs in an article and named section, articles in a chapter and chapters in the textbase during textbase creation. This is to optimise address widths in the index. Non-hierarchic structures are not supported.

6.1.5   Size Limits

Document (record) size should be limited only by available disc storage. *Note limit (if any) on this parameter.*

BASIS Individual documents may not exceed 10k, unless one field has been designated a 'long text' field. In the latter case, documents are chained together (more or less invisibly) so that the only effective limit on overall document size will be that imposed by the available hardware. There may be only one long text field in a document. These restrictions are lifted at Release L.

BRS/Search A document can have up to 65,000 fields, and with a maximum of 65,000 characters per field, this implies a limit of about 4 billion characters.

STATUS No limit - see above for various maxima which textbase manager must define.

Field lengths should be specifiable as variable in length with no maximum. It should be possible to have a document which consists of one field only. *Note limits (if any) on these parameters.*

BASIS The only limit on field length is that implied by the document length limit. A document must have at least one field.

BRS/Search A variable length field can include up to 65,000 characters. A paragraph can contain 1 to 255 sentences. A sentence can contain 1 to 255 indexed words. A word may contain up to 64 characters. BRS/Search defines the first field A minimum of 1 user-defined field is necessary.

STATUS No article has to have either keyed fields or named sections defined. If they are not defined the document in effect has one field either plus or including an article title. Any or all fields can be of any length.

The maximum number of different fields per document, and of occurrences of a given field within a document, should not be less than 125. *Note limits (if any) on these parameters.*

BASIS A document may not have more than 2000 fields. There may be only one occurrence of a given field in a document (but it may be subdivided in various ways). The index may have up to 20 segments, each of which is a file. Assuming a 32-bit word, about 3 million postings are possible for any given term.

BRS/Search A single document can contain up to 65,000 paragraphs or subparagraphs. This may include up to 255 uniquely named fields, with the remainder designated as subparagraphs of those fields.

STATUS Up to 64 named sections are allowed in each textbase and each of these can occur an unlimited number of times. There is no limit on occurrences of keyed fields. No limit on index size, though the create step asks for an estimate.

The maximum length for chosen or generated index strings, thesaurus terms etc. should not be less than 100 characters. *Note limits (if any) on these parameters.*

BASIS Maximum length of index entry (i.e. prefix-separator-entry) is 60 bytes. (120 at Release L)

BRS/Search For index terms, it appears that words are truncated to 96 characters when using a search character set of not more than 40 characters, otherwise it is 64. The BRS BINDING flag automatically inserts hyphens between each word in sentences up to 96 (64) characters in length and thereby indexes the entire sentence as a single searchable word. There is a limit of 127 characters on thesaurus terms (in order to support homonym information).

STATUS Words in STATUS have no size limit but only the first 30 characters are indexed.

The size of the thesaurus and the numbers of stop and go terms should be limited only by hardware considerations. *Note limits (if any) on these parameters. Tabulate file sizes for components of the test datasets.*

BASIS There is no limit on the number of Stop/go word lists which may be defined. The number of entries each can hold depends on the key length used: the recommended maximum is around 400. Beyond this, a thesaurus file should be used, the size of which is limited only by hardware considerations. The file sizes are shown in Table 6.1.

BRS/Search The standard stopword list includes about 70 common words. For each database you can create up to 2 alternate stopword lists of up to 100 words each (with each word up to 64 characters). On request, BRS-Europe will generate systems that will allow up to 1,000 stopwords per list. Goword lists may be implemented via a thesaurus, there appears to be no limits on thesaurus sizes. BRS/Search maintains the database-related files shown in Table 6.2. In Table 6.3 VMS blocks allocated are described as follows:
"Source" is the data used as input to the database
"Text" is TXT0
"Index" is TXIX + DICT + INV0
"Tables" is FORM + INFO. The (optional) reverse dictionary sizes were not included. The Homer database was implemented twice (accent sensitive and accent blind).

STATUS The go term thesaurus is an add-on with no limit to the number of terms. There is no limit to the number of stop words (common words), and words may be designated common words after the textbase has been created. The file sizes are given in Table 6.4.

Table 6.1: BASIS: file sizes (RMS blocks)

	Email	Shake	Homer	MARC
Source	119	104	102	627
Text	147	175	127	479
Index	567	651	1091	1651
Tables	94	53	60	109

Table 6.2: BRS: files used

DICT	The Dictionary File is a list of each searchable word in the database.
RDCT	The (optional) Reverse Dictionary File is a reverse list of each searchable word in the database.
INV0	The Inverted File contains an entry for each searchable word in the database, with pointers to BRS-Assigned document numbers for every record containing that word.
TXIX	The Text Index file is an index to the actual documents contained in the database.
TXT0	the Text File contains the actual text of every document in the database.
INFO	The Information File contains database information used to process searching and printing requests.
FORM	The Database Form File specifies a variety of database- and paragraph-specific information. It is specified at the time of database creation.
STAT	The (optional) Load Statistics File contains database load statistics that result from adding, modifying or deleting documents.

Table 6.3: BRS: file sizes (RMS blocks)

	Email	Shake	Homer (case)	Homer (blind)	MARC
Source	515	308	424	424	710
Text	440	270	298	349	307
Index	624	425	588	549	325
Tables	4	3	4	7	31

Table 6.4: STATUS: file sizes (RMS blocks)

	Email	Shake	Homer (case)	Homer (blind)	MARC
Source	535	695	432	432	373
Text (allocated)	1750	500	2500	2500	750
Text (occupied)	581	331	450	450	511
Con'dnce (alloc)	7500	5000	10000	10000	2750
Con'dnce (occup)	5706	4332	5417	7119	2724
Con'dnce (compress)	2935	2331	2958	2420	2179

6.1.6   Verification

Good indexing techniques are essential to maximise the success of
searches. This success can also depend on verification and control of the
data in certain fields or sub-fields of documents and so we consider the
two together. Facilities should be provided to:

- verify input data in a number of ways. Some examples are:
    - numeric only
    - alphabetic only
    - upper/lower case
    - date - in various forms
    - fixed-length
    - minimum/maximum size
    - presence/absence
    - value dependent upon value in some other part of the document

– pattern matching

Comment on range of validation procedures available

BASIS Can test that items are numeric, alphabetic, within a range, specific value, specific length, conform to various date formats, present or absent, dependent on some other part of document, conform to a pattern. Validation is defined in DDL, and a change requires recompilation of DDL. Existing data can be unloaded and reloaded.

BRS/Search Verification procedures include testing for letters, symbols, numbers, amounts, dates, min/max no. of characters, min/max no. of lines, max line length, valid characters, mask/match items. When using BRS/Demon editor extra validation functions are available, eg the contents of a field can depend on the contents of others, and any thesaurus can be used interactively to validate text and if necessary perform automatic word replacement.

STATUS Validation of keyed fields for data type and of the document structure only.

- allow for fields, sub-fields, to be indexed or not. *Note whether indexing optional for fields*

BASIS Yes

BRS/Search Indexing is optional for fields.

STATUS Yes, since individual named section contents may be excluded from the concordance, as can keyed field values. Text consisting of numeric strings can also be excluded from the indexing process.

- allow for redefinition of indexing requirements. (See also Chapter A.6.) *Note whether indexing redefinable*

BASIS Yes. Utilities are available to rebuild index entries for affected documents.

BRS/Search Yes, but data would generally need re-loading and re-indexing.

STATUS Indexing or concording fields is a Yes or No choice without different ways of achieving it. Common words can be added after creation. You cannot opt later to concord named sections which were previously not concorded or vice versa.

- allow indexing of one or more fields or sub-fields via one or more thesauruses (this is taken to include dictionaries, go-lists and stop-lists). *Determine whether or not thesaural relationships are established at time of indexing. Consider any implications this has on indexing and searching when a thesaurus is modified.*

BASIS If a thesaurus is used to implement term-switching (e.g. index occurrences of 'politician' under 'liar') then any change in the thesaurus will obviously require that the affected field be re-indexed. This also applies if a thesaurus is to be applied retrospectively. Reindexing a single field does not affect the rest of the database.

BRS/Search Indexing of a field via a thesaurus is possible. Thesaural relationships are not established at the time of indexing in that the use of a thesaurus does not force (or allow) words not explicitly in the text to be indexed. Thus, as far as the system's searching capabilities are concerned, a thesaurus can be created or updated independent of the indexing process.

STATUS The go thesaurus is active only during searching. The common word or stop list is active at indexing time and applies to all concorded fields.

- provide by whatever means a wealth of indexing algorithms to allow for the widest range of search specifications, eg to support word proximity searching. Techniques should be provided to deal with:

  - plurals

  - possessives ('s)

  - redefinitions of word boundaries, eg to cater for dealing with hyphenation in more than one way

  - presentation variations such as case, accent and spelling

  - multiple posting, ie indexing a field in a number of ways

  - hidden, escape or noise characters. These should be versatile to allow for searching and display if required.

Notes should be made by implementors of ways in which above are achieved (or not). Any difficulties or undesirable effects as a result of achieving a particular aim should be noted.

BASIS Plural control, suppression of numbers and date conversion are supported, as well as stop-word, go-word, and abbreviation lists. Fields may be indexed in many different ways, using different prefixes. Terms within fields may be indicated by position, relative to start or end of field, or by user-defined delimiter, or by data held in another field of the same document. Reverse indexes can be built to optimise stem matching. Word-level indexing is supported at Release L, but not currently, so some types of search may be slower than others. A 'hidden string' mechanism is provided to suppress indexing of e.g. escape sequences or formatting codes. Other presentational variations require multiple indexing of the data: see for example the Homer database. Case sensitivity is optional at Release L but not currently available. It is also possible to customise indexing by altering the dialogue file, but as only one dialogue file may be in use at any time this may lead to confusion.

BRS/Search Fields may be searchable or non-searchable, displayable or non-displayable. Searchable fields may or may not be declared as full text. Full text implies presence of more than one paragraph in the field and you have to specify the maximum (up to 65,000) at the time of definition. Since, for each word in a field, its position within a sentence and paragraph is known, proximity searching is well-supported. In addition, plural control, double-posting of hyphenated words, automatic hyphenation of short sentences, stopword lists, and thesaurus control are definable. Displayable and non-displayable (but available at update) lists of characters can be defined, as can skip/end-skip sequences, to support hidden strings for word-processing applications, for example. A reverse dictionary can be built to optimise stem searching

STATUS Indexing or concording fields is a Yes or No choice without different ways of achieving it. Word positions are held and this allows full proximity searching including within n or -n words to be supported. A standard set of characters provide word delimiters, and these may be redefined within textbase creation. Certain characters have reserved use within STATUS and can never be included in words to be indexed, eg space, tab, dot, less-than and dollar. Other characters can only be used when enclosed in quotes during search, eg comma and slash. All indexing is case insensitive.

Summary of Section 6.1 The ability to structure the text in a database is a **very important** feature of a package and the evaluations in this section have covered a very wide range of facilities that might be required in an academic environment. All three packages perform well but, overall, BASIS is felt to be the most generally successful here, its main limitations being with regard to the size of the document that can be encompassed and to the limited facilities for proximity searching (when compared to the other two packages). Both BRS/Search and STATUS have serious difficulties with the structure of the Shakespeare text and the validation procedures in STATUS are noticeably less well developed than in the other two. STATUS' limit on key term length was felt to be restrictive. In BRS/Search, changing the indexing requirements generally implies ro loading the database.

6.2   Retrieval functions

6.2.1   Retrieval language

Boolean retrieval language is essential, including such features as :-

- presence/absence of any terms of specified type

- presence/absence of specified terms of any type

- proximity searching

- adequate facilities to encompass variant word-forms and spellings. These should include left and right hand truncation, wild card, accent blind/sensitive, case blind/sensitive, SOUNDEX style phonetic matching.

Carry out tests specified in Appendix A.8 and comment on results.

BASIS Searches are specified using FIND, SCAN or FIND WITHIN commands. The syntax is simple and can be simplified further by intelligent use of defaults. For example, assuming a default field has been specified in the DDL, in hierarchic search mode the user might type just

   FISH
        (to request all documents in which the term FISH appears in the default field somewhere)

   DISPLAY
        (to display — possibly different — default fields for the last set of documents recovered)

   CHIPS
        (to request the subset of the documents last recovered containing the word CHIPS as well)

More complex searches require more complex syntax to avoid ambiguity.

   FIND FLD=FISH AND FLD=CHIPS

   FIND TEXT=FISH AND NOT TEXT=CHIPS

   FIND (DATE LT 1-MARCH OR SITE=VAX) AND TOPIC=VIRUS

Basic syntax is

FIND =*set expr*

where the optional *set* is the number of a previously created document set, *expr* is a search expression in the form *prefix relop value* or a combination of such search expressions using AND OR NOT. *prefix* is a legal prefix for the database; *relop* is a relational operator and *value* a value. Both *prefix* and *value* may contain wildcard characters, which always match 0 to n characters. There is no syntax supporting GREP style regular expressions. All searching is case-blind. The usual arithmetic comparisons are supported for appropriate fields. The context-unit within which multi-term searches (e.g. FISH AND CHIPS) are carried out is defined at load-time and cannot be altered (though it may be disabled: i.e. a search can be made either within a context unit or within a document). FIND WITHIN command can be used to locate co-occurrences within the same context unit, or within n context units; e.g.

FIND WITHIN 2 FISH;CHIPS

locates FISH and CHIPS occurring at most 2 context units apart. More precise proximity matching requires uses of the SCAN command which performs a second pass through the documents recovered (usually) by a previous FIND command. As a bonus, it offers many additional options, some of which are listed below:

SCAN field FISH w<4 CHIPS
  (FISH and CHIPS are separated by up to four words)

SCAN field FISH,CHIPS
  (FISH before CHIPS)

SCAN field FISH ADJ CHIPS
  (FISH adjacent to CHIPS)

SCAN field AB
  (field is absent)

SCAN field=^&&&
  (FIELD consists of a letter followed by 3 digits)

SCAN fld1 GT #fld2
  (contents of FLD2 must be greater than contents of FLD1)

SCAN fld1,fld2 12 BX 20
  (either FLD1 or FLD2 has a value between 12 and 20 exclusive)

SCAN fld(ANY) INC COMPUT*
  (every element of the multiple field FLD includes a word begining COMPUT)

In the list of tests specified, the following would normally require a FIND followed by a SCAN:

- Term *before* or *after* term
- Term *within N terms of* term

- any pattern matching other than simple 'wildcard' style (0 to n characters)

Exact (i.e. case sensitive) matching is not supported, and accent blind matching entails multiple indexing of the text. There is also no way of doing quorum search, other than by clever programming. All other specified tests are easily supported.

BRS/Search The BRS dictionary file for each database contains positional information for every unique word, thus a good deal of word proximity searching is supportable. By default, all the paragraphs (fields) are searched, but you can be selective and restrict searches to fields of interest. In search mode you might type:

FISH
>   (to request all documents containing the word FISH)

FISH.PET.
>   (to request all documents containing the word FISH in the PET paragraph, FISH[PET] is an alternative)

FISH..PET.
>   (to request all documents containing the word FISH in any paragraph other than the PET paragraph, FISH[-PET] is an alternative)

FISH.PET,MENU.
>   (to request all documents containing the word FISH in the PET or MENU paragraphs)

FISH AND CHIPS
>   (to retrieve all documents with FISH and CHIPS in the same document)

FISH OR CHIPS
>   (to retrieve all documents with FISH or CHIPS in the same document)

FISH XOR CHIPS
>   (to retrieve all documents with FISH or CHIPS, but not both, in the same document)

FISH NOT CHIPS
>   (to retrieve all documents with FISH in the document, but not CHIPS)

FISH SAME CHIPS
>   (to retrieve all documents with FISH and CHIPS in the same paragraph)

FISH NOT SAME CHIPS
>   (to retrieve all documents with FISH in the paragraph, but not CHIPS)

FISH WITH CHIPS
> (to retrieve all documents with FISH and CHIPS in the same sentence)

FISH ADJ CHIPS
> (to retrieve all documents with FISH followed by CHIPS in the same sentence)

FISH NEAR CHIPS
> (to retrieve all documents with FISH followed by CHIPS or CHIPS followed by FISH in the same sentence)

Note that the ADJ and NEAR operators normally imply that keywords are adjacent to one another. These definitions can be modified with SET NEARLEVEL or SET ADJLEVEL. Thus, for example:

SET NEARLEVEL = 3

FISH NEAR CHIPS
> (will retrieve all documents with CHIPS within 3 words of FISH. STOPWORDS are not counted)

Case sensitive searching is not possible, however if you wished to generally search a database in this way you could define a language table that did not map lower case letters onto upper case. This would have to be done before database loading (or re-loading) and could not be switched off. Pattern matching facilities include:

FISH$
> (will retrieve all documents with words beginning with FISH)

$FISH
> (will retrieve all documents with words ending with FISH)

$FISH$
> (will retrieve all documents with FISH embedded within. Two way truncation takes considerable processing time)

F$ISH
> (will retrieve all documents with an embedded character string after F, before ISH)

Multiple character restrictions can be placed, eg

FISH$2
> (will retrieve documents containing FISH, FISHY, FISHES, but not FISHING or any terms with more than 2 characters following FISH)

Single character restrictions can be placed, eg

FISH?
> (will retrieve documents containing a five character word beginning with FISH, eg FISHY but not FISH. ? can be embedded, eg WOM?N and can be used many times)

STATUS The following list shows how the sample queries might be attempted:

Q FISH ?
> (to request all documents containing the word FISH)

Q FISH + CHIPS ?
> (to request documents containing the words FISH and CHIPS in same article)

Q (FISH + CHIPS) @ TITLE ?
> (to request documents containing the words FISH and CHIPS in same named section)

Q FISH//CHIPS ?
> (to request documents containing the words FISH and CHIPS in same paragraph)

Q FISH CHIPS ?
> (to request documents containing the word FISH directly preceding CHIPS)

Q FISH/1,999/CHIPS ?
> (to request documents containing the word FISH before CHIPS in same paragraph)

Q CHIPS FISH ?
> (to request documents containing the word FISH directly following CHIPS)

Q CHIPS/1,999/FISH ?
> (to request documents containing the word FISH directly following CHIPS in same paragraph)

Q FISH/-m,n/CHIPS ?
> (to request documents containing the word FISH within m words preceding and n words following word CHIPS)

Q FISH,CHIPS ?
> (to request documents containing either FISH or CHIPS)

Q FISH - CHIPS ?
> (to request documents containing word FISH except those also containing CHIPS)

Q FISH* ?
> (to request document containing words beginning with characters FISH followed by 0 to n other characters. This is the only truncation possible in a concordance search. Left hand and single character truncation possible onlt in search of keyed fields or a SCAN search, and internal truncation with SCAN only.)

Q #REF FISH!! ?
> (to request documents containing a keyed field (REF) beginning FISH followed by two additional characters)

    Q #REF FISH!* ?
        (to request documents containing a keyed field (REF) beginning
        FISH followed by at least one two additional character)

    Q #REF *FISH* ?
        (to request documents containing a keyed field (REF) containing
        FISH preceded and followed by any characters)

    Q #KEY > 5 ?
        (to request documents containing a keyed field (KEY) with value
        more than 5. Arithmetic comparisons are possible in keyed fields
        only.)

Case insensitive searching is the normal mode of operation. Exact case
matching is not possible except in STATUS IQ (see above) where it is
essential. Similarly accent blind searching is not possible in the same
textbase. A decision must be taken to include or exclude accent
characters. In the example given the various versions could be declared as
synonyms and the accent characters concorded. The SUBQ command
carries out all the above queries on the current retrieved list. Boolean
logic is carried out left to right with nested brackets permitted to clarify
order of operations. Brackets nested to 20 levels were understood. The
maximum length of search expressions is 1920 characters.

6.2.2   Manipulating retrievals

It should be possible to save, re-order, re-select from and combine
retrieved document sets, possibly from different databases. All set
operations (union, intersection, difference) should be supported. All
document sets made active during a session (or saved from a previous
session) should be accessible in this way. *Note availability of save,
re-order, re-select from and combine. Note which operators supported.
Note if restricted to retrievals in current session.*

BASIS Document sets can be saved and re-used. Items may be sorted, re-
selected from, and combined using all standard Boolean operations. Only
one database can be opened at a time however.

BRS/Search Everything is possible , except for 'simultaneous' multi-db
retrieval in any interface other than the Searchmate interface. In Release 5
of BRS it will be possible to search up to 16 databases simultaneously.

STATUS STATUS uses the concept of the current document collection.
Subqueries may be generated from the current retrieved list, and you can
afterwards swap back to the original list (SWOPRL). Sets retrieved
earlier in the present session are not available without being re-formed.

One way of achieving this is to use temporary macros (commands QSTORE and QSTOP). The saving of the sets needs to be foreseen. In addition articles which have type A keyed fields defined can have retrieval lists written to a file and rebuilt later through the the BUILDRL command. Retrievals possible only from the selected textbase; however different chapters within the same textbase provide the capability for storing different material within the same search environment.
Re-ordering of retrieved documents is possible via keyed fields only.

6.2.3   Scoring for relevance

It should also be possible to rank documents in terms of the similarity of their contents, and retrieve documents with a "relevance factor" greater than some specified threshold. *Note whether features exist to "tag" document in this way with a user or system-defined score, and (if so) what facilities exist for manipulating the score as a new field.*

BASIS No specific features provided for this.

BRS/Search Nothing is available, but when viewing documents from a document set, interesting documents can be 'tagged' and subsequently printed, for example. In Release 5, weighted displays are permitted where the documents with the highest number of 'hits' are printed first.

STATUS The IQ front end announced and about to be released in the UK provides a ranking algorithm for retrieved records which is produced using expert system techniques. It also provides a natural language query interface from which noise words are excluded and word relationships imposed. The retrieved records are then compared with a theoretical density which has been calculated and a relevance presented as a percentage. This product has been seen but was not part of the evaluated STATUS product. It has been in use in USA and Australia for a year.

6.2.4   Macros and SDI

Users should be able to define and maintain re-usable macros and search profiles. An SDI (Selective Dissemination of Information) capability is also desirable. This would enable users to search a database using the same criteria at regular intervals, retrieving only documents that have been added to the database since the last search was made. *Attempt to create macros as specified in Appendix A.9, below. Comment on ease of definition and convenience in use. Note whether SDI feature available, and if so carry out SDI test procedure also specified in Appendix A.9.*

BASIS A profile XOR was defined and implemented in about ten minutes. The source is given in Figure 6.1. In principle, writing a similar profile to generate the search expressions for a Quorum search would be equally feasible. There are loop expressions in BML (though no array facilities) so it should be generalisable. It would be fairly time consuming to run for anything but a trivial number of search terms however. A more efficient solution would probably be to write the code in a 3GL and use the HLI. It is possible to nominate a profile (BML program) to be run whenever a partkicular user signs on to the system. To implement an SDI capability it would also be necessary to update some globally accessible field of the database with the date of last access, as no built in facility is provided for this purpose.

BRS/Search The save-search capability will let you save a sequence of search statements or files for execution at a later time. Saved searches are not necessarily tied to any particular database. Using the Native mode interface, the XOR test was implemented and run with the following three lines:

```
001 xor 002
..save xortest
..exec xortest fish chips
```

You can do a little more than this with the save search capability alone. For example, comments can be saved within a save search and these may be echoed on execution, or not, and default arguments can be defined. However more sophistication would require the use of the MNS system (eg to prompt for arguments). The quorum search could be attempted with MNS (but was not). You can set up a database-specific save search that is automatically executed when anyone signs into that database. You can also set up a user-specific save search that is automatically executed when a particular user signs onto the Native Mode interface.

STATUS Macros in STATUS provide a method of storing sequences of STATUS commands and queries for either private or more general use. The facilities include conditionals, user input during execution, message interception and parameterisation. Macro XOR contains

```
Q (($1,$2)-($1 + $2)) ?
```

It is run by

```
XOR FISH;CHIPS
```

It is possible to write a STATUS macro, say THREEOF5 which contains

```
Q
($1+$2+$3),($1+$2+$4),($1+$2+$5),($1+$3+$4),
($1+$3+$5),($1+$4+$5),($2+$3+$4),
($2+$3+$5),($2+$4+$5),($3+$4+$5) ?
```

Figure 6.1: BASIS : The XOR macro

```
*PFL* XOR
l1:erase
tell(2)              EXCLUSIVE-OR  MACRO TEST
tell(2)
l2: ask/lv fld Which prefix do you wish to search?
if(fld.eqc.$null) then
   list prefix
   jump l2
endif
l3: ask/lv t1 Please enter FIRST term  ========>
jumpif (t1.eqc.$null) l3
l4: ask/lv t2 Please enter SECOND term ========>
jumpif (t2.eqc.$null) l4:
tell(3)       Thank you...
assign/lv t1=!fld!=!t1!
assign/lv t2=!fld!=!t2!
find (!t1! or !t2!) and not (!t1! and !t2!)
```

Run by
THREEOF5 FISH;CHIPS;PEAS;VINEGAR;SALT
However, STATUS IQ (see above) provides routinely a listing of records
which contain varying numbers of the search tokens input and some
measure of their relevance. This is the best STATUS approach to this
need. Named stored question macros can be created and maintained.
They process the entire database, and for SDI purposes a method of
adding an indicator of the date of addition must be found. A macro to
carry out SDI on a textbase which contains a keyed field **#RECDATE** is
provided with the STATUS demonstration system.

6.2.5   Browsing

It is essential to be able to browse forward and back within retrieved
documents. *Note whether browsing possible.*

BASIS All fields of documents can be displayed selectively. Browsing within a
field is available for 'long text' fields only; retrieved context units can be
highlighted, and can move to next hit within field.

BRS/Search Any document set can be selected. Many options are available in the supplied interfaces. All fields of a document can be displayed, fields can be displayed selectively, can be displayed only if the search term(s) appears within them, can be ordered, etc. Documents from within a set can be selected. Browsing in the sense of moving forwards and backwards through a document is supported. Search terms are highlighted.

STATUS A series of commands allows browsing within a retrieved document, and additional commands identify the location of the search term(s) without the need to display the whole article. Such commands include FORWARD, BACK, CONTEXT and ZOOM (for textbase browsing) and the STRING and DP commands (for document browsing). In addition the page breaking on the screen can be controlled by the user, and parts of the document skipped. Browsing with FORWARD and BACK does not require a current retrieved list to operate, and allows inter-document browsing. This is also possible with a single keystroke in full screen display mode (see below). Any non-indexed text is retrieved via the SCAN and NOTSCAN commands or by ZOOMing to a text string which was not part of the original query.

6.2.6 Logging

It should be possible to maintain and manipulate a log of interactive sessions. It should also be possible to prepare queries for submission to a background process. *Note whether session log-file available and existence of any tools operating on these files. Note whether query files can be run in batch.*

BASIS Session can be saved and replayed at any point. No specific features for running files in batch: user must supply all of interactive session in a file.

BRS/Search Log-files or save-searches can be kept, edited and purged. They can be re-run at any time and although nothing is directly provided to automate this it would not be difficult to achieve on most systems. It is possible to have a save-set run when a user logs on, or when a particular database is accessed.

STATUS Single queries can be read from files (QF command); this is part of a STATUS feature called routing which also allows output destinations to be controlled. Any session started up with the /LOG qualifier is logged. Input and output can optionally be logged in separate files or not at all. If input is logged separately it is possible to use this log to restart a session to reach a particular point for continuation.

Summary of Section 6.2 This again is a **very important** feature and the tests have been accordingly detailed. There is a range of pluses and minuses here, e.g., STATUS does not offer set processing capabilities but has a very well developed set of browsing features; the latter is an area where BASIS performs rather poorly but this package provides the best session logging facilities. Overall, we judge that BRS/Search offers the best overall mix of functions.

6.3 Output functions

6.3.1 Report writer

Report format should be fully user-specifiable, in layout, page headings, control of duplicates etc. *Note whether these features exist and any obvious limitations.*

BASIS Report writer supports most features of 3GL programming language (variables, loops, procedures etc.). Formatting is reminiscent of Fortran. No specific features for duplicate suppression etc.

BRS/Search A wide variety of display choices is available by default. In addition, the Print-Time Formatting Guide defines how customised output formats can be built. Once defined, the definitions can be saved and shared by all users if necessary. Page layout can be controlled, headers, footers and dates inserted. A simple conditional printing statement allows for printing only if certain conditions apply (eg only if particular fields exist in a document). Nothing is provided to control duplicates.

STATUS At the simpler end the order of named sections and main text can be changed, and reports can include subsets of the full record. Layouts and margins are user specifiable. The LAYOUT command controls the indenting of first lines of paragraphs, subsequent lines, section names and text on same line as section name. The LINESIZE command controls output line length. BREAK specifies screen page length. Macros and STATUS markers can also be used in combination to aid report layout definition. A scrollable (four way) display screen controlled by function keys is available in SCREEN PAGE mode. An additional report generator is an add-on to the core STATUS software. This allows data to be output into proformas and is used for such applications as mail shots and routine formatted reports. This tool also has more reporting arithmetic available than standard STATUS.

It should be possible to save report specifications for re-use with different document sets within the same or different databases. *Note whether report specs can be saved and, if so, whether the spec is in an external file which can be listed, edited etc with standard tools.*

BASIS Report specification is usually saved as an external file, compiled and run. It can be listed edited etc with standard tools.

BRS/Search Print formats can be saved and edited. It is in standard text form and so can be accessed external to BRS/Search.

STATUS The formats can be saved as STATUS macros which can be edited and used in other textbases. All files used in the STATUS report generator are also editable.

6.3.2 Routing output

Ability to route output to printer, standard text (e.g. ASCII or EBCDIC) file, word processor or specialist device (possibly with user-supplied conversion on output, e.g. to produce nonstandard characters) or to a mail server. *Note*

- *whether output can be sent to external file*

- *existence of postprocessing facilities and (if so) whether such facilities include the execution of user-specified procedures.*

BASIS Output can be sent to any standard VMS output route. No specific postprocessing facilities provided. No CALL interface from report writer.

BRS/Search Output can be directed to any available queue (printer or batch) or a file. Thus a job could be submitted to a batch queue and this job could generate mail messages. Printer characteristics and formatting information can be defined for available printers (cf terminal characteristics). Support for WordPerfect documents is provided at Release 5.

STATUS Output can be routed to printers, standard text files (ASCII or EBCDIC) and supported display devices. No post processing facilities as described exist within STATUS itself, though interfaces between Wordperfect and STATUS, for example, have been developed as special facilities for individual users.

6.3.3 Formatting

It is, for certain applications, vital to be able to make data take on a standard structure on output: for example, to be able to impose MARC or SGML structure on data which has been stored in a different format. *Note whether facilities exist to define such an output conversion and whether any are available as standard.*

BASIS Not specifically provided

BRS/Search This is possible, but nothing is provided, by default.

STATUS No specific routines available for MARC, SGML or word processing formatted output (see above).

Summary of Section 6.3 Once a search has been carried out, it is **important** that the output can be processed subsequently. There is little to choose here for three of the sets of tests; however, BRS/Search does allow the definition of printing characteristics and of formatting information.

6.4 Control of terminology

The tests discussed in this section relate to the test thesaurus described in Appendix A.7.

6.4.1 Thesaurus

An integrated thesaurus is felt to be an essential component of the system. It should be possible selectively to control terms entering the database and to maintain authority files. Terminology control features of this kind should be optional and once introduced reversible with minimal upheaval. *In particular note*

- *richness of thesaurus structure (broader term, related term, narrower term, synonym, preferred term, etc)*

  BASIS Standard ANSI relations are all supported.

BRS/Search This follows the published ANSI standard and appears a fairly complete implementation.

STATUS Supports synonyms, broader, narrower, related, and see terms, and scope notes. Synonyms only are supported in the standard STATUS product, while all are supported in the thesaurus handler which is an add-on to main STATUS but has been included in the evaluated product. It is not possible to relate a narrower term to two broader terms; the narrow term must be entered twice.

- *whether synonym and preferred term conversions are performed automatically for the user*

  BASIS Conversion (term-switching) at query time is carried out automatically, but can be disabled.

  BRS/Search You can set (or not set) the system to perform automatic replacement of non- preferred terms with preferred terms when using the Native and Searchmate interfaces. This is available in MNS also. Searching with the thesaurus can use any relationship you specify, including synonyms.

  STATUS Conversion of synonyms at query time is not automatic and requires the '&' symbol to occur within the query unless queries are captured by a STATUS macro. Under STATUS IQ (see above) the term extension is automatic.

- *ease with which new terms can be added, old ones removed and existing relationships changed*

  BASIS Thesaurus manipulation is carried out from BML, and is thus no more or less difficult than anything else.

  BRS/Search A thesaurus can be maintained via menu-driven software.

  STATUS Synonyms are easy to create within a textbase. Within the thesaurus handler it is easy to add and delete terms. Changing is done by deletion followed by add.

- *ease of creation of new thesaurus*

  BASIS Thesaurus is loaded in batch from simple ASCII file in fairly obvious format.

  BRS/Search Creation is possible either online, via menus or more likely by utility programs using data from a file. Programs exists to verify the thesaurus structure and to build the thesaurus. The small test thesaurus was very straightforwardly created via the menu interface. A thesaurus verification procedure exists to validate reciprocating relationships of terms in the thesaurus. This may need to be run a number of times to achieve total correctness of a thesaurus.

STATUS The thesaurus must be created once the textbase is already in existence. It is intended to be an interactive operation, but can be manipulated to operate in batch; the test thesaurus was created in batch.

- *whether the thesaurus by default is always active and enforcing integrity during both retrieval and update*

BASIS Use of thesaurus during validation is optional (but cannot be switched without recompilation of DDL).

BRS/Search The use of a thesaurus at validation (input) is specified at the time of database definition (fields may be thesaurus controlled or not). At search time, you can choose to use a thesaurus, or not. (In native mode the commands ..WHAT THESAURUS and ..SET THESAURUS = thesname are used).

STATUS No. The thesaurus is called up using a qualifier with the 'STATUS' command and requires the '&' character to be present in a query.

- *whether the thesaurus can be by-passed in retrieval or update as a temporary measure to relax integrity constraints*

BASIS Depending whether thesaurus control has been specified as optional or mandatory, it may be necessary to recompile the DDL to change the status of thesaurus control for a particular field.

BRS/Search Use of a thesaurus can be bypassed at both stages. Data validation can be avoided and searching via a thesaurus is switchable.

STATUS Not used in update. It is bypassed in retrieval by omitting the '&' character.

- *how easy it is for the thesaurus to be permanently disabled*

BASIS Depending whether thesaurus control has been specified as optional or mandatory, it may be necessary to recompile the DDL to change the status of thesaurus control for a particular field.

BRS/Search Fairly easy, best to change database definition probably for input stage.

STATUS Not used in update. Switch off by selecting the textbase without the thesaurus qualifier or leaving out the '&' character.

- *actions available when an entered term fails to match the thesaurus (fatal, warning, re-try, nature of messages)*

BASIS The DDL specifies for a thesaurus-controlled field (as indeed for all validation procedures) whether the action on error should be to permit the user to over-ride the failure, or whether the test must be satisfied. Appropriate messages may be specified in the DDL in either case.

BRS/Search Depending on the method of update, all options are available.

STATUS Not used in update. During query there are 0 hits and messages seen may be intercepted through a macro.

- *whether able to declare a thesaurus as specific to given field(s), to use more than one thesaurus per database*

BASIS Thesaurus can be specified for particular field. No limit on number of thesauri that can be used in database.

BRS/Search Individual fields can be thesaurus controlled. More than one thesaurus can be used per database.

STATUS Synonyms can be invoked as specific to a named section. Its use can be limited to a particular field by the need to use the '&' character to invoke it, or its application can be controlled by macros. Only one thesaurus available per textbase.

- *whether able to invoke a specific thesaurus for augmenting queries*

BASIS Yes.

BRS/Search Yes.

STATUS Only one thesaurus available per textbase.

- *whether able to nominate a specific relation in order to expand the terms to be included in a query*

BASIS Yes.

BRS/Search Yes.

STATUS Yes either from an offered list or set with the WINDOW command.

- *in the case of a hierarchic relation, whether able to limit the number of levels to be incorporated in any expansion of a term list*

BASIS Only one level at a time.

BRS/Search A narrower term (NT) is itself a lead term (LT), but there can be no automatic use of this fact in expansion of a term list. There appears to be no other limits imposed.

STATUS Yes through the WINDOW command. Different levels for different relationships available.

- *methods available for displaying the thesaurus to users and administrators*

    BASIS Extensive browse facilities for inspecting Thesaurus from BML. Also TFPRNT utility for producing full report on Thesaurus contents.

    BRS/Search Yes, either in search mode or the whole thesaurus via a utility program (BRSTHVFY).

    STATUS Yes ; one level at a time from a given word.

6.4.2   Index

Index terms should be retrievable and displayable in the same way as documents, preferably using the same commands and utilities. *Note any facilities for extracting and displaying indexes and index terms.*

BASIS Index can be inspected using LOOK command in BML. Document sets can be constructed directly from the output of this command (e.g. all documents indexed by a particular arbitrary collection of terms). Primary key of index is not term but a prefix, usually indicating field in which it occurs. This (or the term, or both) can be wildcarded. A separate utility, IFPRNT, can be used to dump contents of all or part of index, but has no special formatting capabilities.

BRS/Search A reasonably full set of options is available here. ROOT displays a list of words that begin with a particular word root. PREF displays a list of words that end with a particular word ending. EXPAND displays a number of words alphabetically preceding or following a particular word. Note that (by default) the index terms so displayed are done so independently of the fields in which they occur. The program BRSLOAD has a number of useful options including -wordlist, which will simply give you all the words in the dictionary, (users could use this to post-validate words appearing in a database) and -wordstat, that gives much more detailed information.

STATUS The FREQ command allows the user to look at the frequencies of any term including wild-carded terms in the concordance, but is not useful for index browsing. Only users with full read privilege can use the command. Similarly FREQ #* looks at occurrences of keyed fields. If a thesaurus is available it is possible to mark a list of terms from it for search and to use this in a query or build it into a macro for future use. The STFREQ utility provides a textbase manager with a list of all terms in a database concordance together with their frequency of use.

Summary of Section 6.4 A thesaurus provides an **important** way of controlling vocabulary usage in a free text database and there is very little difference between the packages in most of the tests under this heading. The only comments to be made here are with regard to STATUS, which handles hierarchic relationships particularly well but then allows only one thesaurus per database and offers less index browsing facilities than the others. Also, the thesaurus cannot be active during update.

6.5 Updating facilities

6.5.1 Locking

Appropriate locking procedures are essential to maintain database consistency when concurrent accesses to the database are permitted. Although real-time updating may not generally be required, it is important that users be warned when documents marked for update are recovered in their non-updated state. *Note whether update strategies used by package can allow users access to obsolescent/inconsistent data.*

BASIS No realtime update. Documents are locked to prevent simultaneous update. All updates are staged in queuefile; enqueued updates are applied in the order they are found in the queue. Update utilities look for documents in the queue before taking them from database so this should not lead to inconsistency. The queue can also (optionally) be searched, by sequential scan only, before indexes are updated. Indexed access will continue to see non- updated data, so users need to be aware of the way updates are performed. Real time update is available at Release L, which will also support record level locking, transaction control, journal rollback etc.

BRS/Search Documents that are being edited are locked from other users wishing to update them. After editing and validation, the documents are placed on a queue and submitted to the update process. This may be in so-called real-time mode or batch mode. After the update process is finished, the documents are unlocked to permit subsequent updating. Documents may be extracted into a standard text file, edited using any editor and then reloaded using the BRSLOAD program. In this case there is no guarantee that an original document has not been independently edited more than once, and so, without care, one or more 'updates' could be lost. Users with update privilege may however be given the ability to use the BRSLOCK program to lock documents that are being updated in this way.

STATUS In contrast with systems which simply allow on-line spawning of a batch update, STATUS allows online updating, ie multi-user search, display and editing can continue while the index is being updated. It can carry out real time or batch updating. Updates are held in an amendment file prior to update, and this can be accessed by users. Update may be performed globally or selectively by user, and on-line updates and batch can be managed separately. Record locking prevents users clashing when updating a record, and in addition STATUS reports to the user when an item is in process of edit when it displays it in its pre-edited state. Accepted records are immediately available for browsing and the amendment list(s) can be viewed.

6.5.2   Validation

As many of the usual validation procedures as possible should be performed at the time update is requested (i.e. before indexes are rebuilt). Examples include range and integrity checks, controlled vocabulary checking. *Note what validation procedures are available before updates are committed.*

BASIS Interactive updates are validated before they are committed to the queuefile. Batch updates can be validated and enqueued as two distinct operations.

BRS/Search All the validation criteria you define for a field are used to check field contents before loading. Interactive updates are therefore validated before loading. When using the BRS/Search programs directly BRSVFY will validate data. BRSLOAD will load it.

STATUS Input records are validated during the ENLARGE stage prior to indexing. Very little validation of contents is available, mainly of document structure and marking. STATUS automatically adds some missing text markers. The recommended method of validation is by interactive input when the files are already clean before they are presented to STATUS. There is a fast text input option which loads text without most validation checks.

Data which fail validation checks should be made available for subsequent correction (e.g. by being written to a special file). *Note whether documents failing validation can be diverted to file for subsequent correction and re-entry.*

BASIS Bad transactions remain in the queue file with a special tag, and can be extracted for correction.

BRS/Search The BRS/Search validation program is not complicated. When the BRSVFY program is used directly and if data fails verification, errors are diagnosed and you have to make corrections. When interactive updates fail validation, you have the opportunity to re-edit. The lines of input data that have failed validation are clearly identified in that comment lines that explain the nature of the error are inserted at the point of failure.

STATUS Yes during interactive article entry. Otherwise you are provided with article titles which need correction.

It is useful to have the facility to over-ride validation checks: i.e. to decide (usually interactively) that particular cases of failure can be admitted to the database. *Note whether checks can be overridden.*

BASIS DDL defines for each validation test whether it is over-ridable or not.

BRS/Search Yes, anyone with permission to update can override validation checks. If you try to load unverified data, or data that has failed verification, you will be warned of the fact but can override and insist on data being loaded. Note that the user updating the database and the database owner are informed, via mail messages, of updates to the database (this includes error reports).

STATUS No since it is normally a problem in text marking or structure.

6.5.3 Re-indexing

Index rebuilding should be unnecessary during normal updating procedures. There should however be utilities to rebalance or repair corrupt or unbalanced indexes. *Note whether indexes rebuilt (as opposed to altered) on update. Comment on existence, power and convenience of index-handling utilities to:*

- *Rebalance*

- *Repair automatically*

- *Implement user-specified patches*

Consult suppliers and reference sites, enquiring particularly about cpu times and changes in disc storage used.

BASIS No specific utilities exist to rebuild indexes. File organisation is such that rebalancing is unlikely to be needed. IFPRNT can be used to dump, delete, or restore index segments. QFCOPY can be used to selectively delete or compress transactions in the queuefile.

BRS/Search The BRSLOAD program (option -analyze) aims to assist in making decisions about reorganisation of database files and another option of the BRSLOAD program will reorganise index files.

STATUS The index is altered not rebuilt during update. There are a series of STATUS utilities for rebuilding, fixing corruption, and file compression. These are the STATUS Transfer Programs.

6.5.4   Editing

Use of standard interfaces (e.g. available operating system editor) to modify retrieved documents is desirable; the function of any built in editor should not be less than that of e.g. the VAX VMS editor EDT. *Note whether call-out would allow use of standard editor; note existence of any built-in editor and (if any) comment [briefly] on its functionality. Note whether call-out to standard editor can be made transparent to the user.*

BASIS Access to system editor for update of documents not specifically provided but could be built in quite easily using existing interfaces. Two editors provided, one operating in line mode and the other in screen mode. At present, both have deficiencies (e.g. SCREEN cannot handle long text fields at all), though considerable improvements are promised at Release L.

BRS/Search An editor called BRS-Demon is available, however any system editor can be used.

STATUS EDT can be accessed through STATUS macros to manipulate documents one at a time. The edited document is then added to the amendment list. STATUS also provides its own line editor commands for extending and changing articles already in the database. This may be used in macros to provide a global editing facility on-line for batches of records.

6.5.5 Input formats

A wide variety of "raw" input formats should be supported for batch loading of documents. These should include commonly-used word-processor output, SGML style markup, straight ASCII files, MARC format files, output from other Free Text packages etc. Any special markup characters used in the raw input format should be re-definable. *Note range of formats handled.*

BASIS A variety of input formats can be defined. Same input file can use different input formats. No specific formats (e.g. MARC, SGML) supported, but easily definable. Documents can be loaded straight from word processor output, provided that layout is reasonably consistent.

BRS/Search Only relatively simple input formats are employed: you must define an input label of up to 24 characters that uniquely identifies the start of a field.

STATUS Special character markers are necessary for batch loading of STATUS documents, normally a sequence beginning "$$", to indicate the document structure, and presence of named sections or keyed fields. HCP say that STATUS can support production of such a format through tools such as FMS and TDMS, and that SGML-style marking is used in integrations of STATUS with office automation products.

Summary of Section 6.5 The updating of a database, as new records come in or as old ones have to be modified in some way, is an **important** feature. There is again little to choose between the packages. BASIS does not provide any real-time updating capability but compensates for this in the range of inputs that can be accommodated. STATUS handles records that fail validation less well than the other two packages.

6.6 Recovery

The ability of the system to recover from hardware and software failures should be comparable with those available for conventional database systems, and must be sufficient to cope with textbases for which it is impractical to consider total reconstruction. In general, this is a matter of repairing corrupt and/or inconsistent files. The tools required range from complex "automatic" repair utilities to simpler facilities to generate diagnostic dumps and implement user-specified patches (see the discussion of updating, above). *Comment on availability and power of tools. Consult reference sites for user experiences.*

BASIS A journal file is maintained to secure the queue file. The recommended procedure is to backup the queue file and initialise the journal file before any major updates are processed. In the event of corruption of the queue file, the journal can then be used to rollforward the queuefile from the backup. Rollback (to undo transactions) is not available. In the event of corruption of the headfile or indexfile, the only tools available are to delete and restore individual segments, re-applying any relevant transactions in the queue file. This places considerable onus on the DBA to maintain relevant backups and to apply updates in a controlled manner. At Release L full journalling (with before and after images and selective rollback) is supported, which should reduce this load considerably.

BRS/Search You are recommended to backup a changing database frequently. In the event of system failure, records may be locked. These can be identified by the system manager and unlocked using the BRSLOCK program. There is no journal file utility or anything sophisticated in the way of recovery tools. In Release 5, checkpoint/restart facilities have been introduced so that BRSLOAD can be restarted from the last valid document if a machine (for example) crashes or runs out of disc space.

STATUS The RECOVER command available to textbase managers identifies the record with amendment state 'update in progress' and either completes or reverses the update processing performed. UPDATE command is then issued again. Any amendments completed or any not started will be unaffected by the recovery. Documents amended already are available for search before recovery.

Summary of Section 6.6 It is **important** that the database should be recoverable from software or hardware failures; there are currently few tools provided with BRS/Search to cover such occurrences.

6.7 Privacy and security

This may be considered in terms of three main dimensions:

- The *access mode*, divisible into hit, read, write, modify, delete. We can describe these as follows:

Hit the user can (in some way, such as counting) observe that a
data item matches a criterion

Read the user can read a data item (the absence of Hit or Read
permission may be referred to as *masking*)

Write the user can enter a new item of the specified type

Modify the user can change an existing item

Delete the user can remove an item from the database

Note whether this or comparable level of detail supported.

BASIS Access control is implemented by comparing a security code
(associated with some part of a document) with the security code
associated with a user's id. If a document or prefix can be accessed
at all, an additional level of protection can also be specified,
permitting read only, add only, modify or full access.

BRS/Search Users and databases are assigned privilege levels ranging
from 1-255 within groups 1-256. In order to search a database a
user's privilege level for the particular database group must be equal
to or greater than the corresponding database searching privilege
level. The same goes for editing, but in addition each database can
have separate edit privilege levels to control access to addition, edit
and delete functions. Additional security passwords may be used for
both databases and users. Commands can be removed to prohibit
access by individual users. Users can be given permission to run
specified utility programs.

STATUS Access modes are read and write with levels specifiable
between 0 and 32767. Users with no privilege do not see hit counts,
and are not notified of the existence of items they are not allowed to
see. Deletion of items limited to designated textbase managers of
which there may be more than one. Amend actions require write
privileges.

- The types of *user classes* which can be specified: one would
normally expect to be able to group users into broad categories,
perhaps of a hierarchical nature, such as

  - the individual
  - all those in a particular user group
  - all users

and to be able to specify access permissions in terms of these
classes. It is also useful to be able to specify access in terms of *ad
hoc* lists of individual users. *Note whether access specifiable in terms
of user-group and/or user-lists.*

BASIS Within one database, the comparison used to establish access
may be one of: equality; arithmetically greater; bit matching. This
gives considerable flexibility in the way groups of ids may be made
up. All user ids, access codes and passwords are defined in the DDL,
unless an external access control database is used, which is a
site-specific option.

BRS/Search Users must be registered and given access rights to
databases as described above. Generally, a userid cannot be used by
more than one person at once, but so-called anonymous ids can be
shared. The database and user privilege levels described above allow
for reasonably flexible regimes.

STATUS Each individual user of a textbase must be registered and
given levels of access value rights for read and write.

- The types of data item to which different access permissions may be
  attached. Combinations of user and mode should be specifiable at
  document level (minimum requirement) and at lower levels :
  horizontal, such as the paragraph; and vertical, such as the field
  (desirable). It is also useful to be able to specify masking on a data
  criterion (for example, to make the visibility of salaries depend on
  their magnitude). It should also be possible to specify access
  permissions for utilities and macros. *Note extent to which these
  points are met.*

  BASIS Access can be controlled to an indexing prefix, to specific
  documents, or to specific fields of all documents. Macros (profiles)
  etc. can be either specific to the current ID or global. Creation of
  globally available macros is a system-owner privilege. Value-based
  access-control is not directly supported.

  BRS/Search A system administrator can lock a document to prohibit
  editing. Display privilege can be controlled at the paragraph (field)
  level. Specific documents can be protected. Search level security
  makes it possible to prevent a user from obtaining a search result if
  the search term occurs in a document for which the user is not
  privileged.

  STATUS Chapter, article (body of document), article title and named
  section level security available. Value security is not truly available
  but could be implemented via a macro.

Summary of Section 6.7 It is **important** that access to stored data is
restricted to those who are entitled. All of the packages provide a
satisfactory range of procedures here.

6.8 Administration issues

In general, the software may be used by workers who are either acting individually or as members of groups. Within groups, there will be a need for some common method of controlling access to a shared database and for allocating responsibility for that database. Between groups and individuals who are using the same machine for different projects there will be a need for the system manager to be able to allocate and control resources — the most important of which is likely to be filestore in a university environment. These considerations give rise to a number of detailed points.

- It is important that the filestore occupied by each database on a machine is allocated its own filespace which can be charged to the individual or group responsible for that database (rather than, say, occupying a share of a large common area allocated to the applications package as a whole). *Note arrangements for allocation of filespace to different applications.*

  BASIS All components of a database are individual VMS files chargeable in the same way as any other.

  BRS/Search By default, all files are placed in a single hierarchical structure and under VMS you could therefore avoid charging users for filespace. The location of database files can however be specified explicitly and so the usual disk quota rules would apply

  STATUS A textbase consists of four files access logically under VMS. Their ownership and location is therefore controlled in the same way as any other VMS file.

- It is useful if the system allows the role of Database Administrator (DBA) to be occupied by a number of individuals so that each group of workers, or each individual worker, can take responsibility for their own database(s). Equally, it may be useful for a central DBA to be able to assume responsibility for all of the databases in a particular area. *Note flexibility of arrangements for allocation of DBA responsibilities.*

  BASIS No need for central DBA, though one is advisable.

  BRS/Search The BRS/Search system administrator controls the use of all BRS/Search databases. Users can be given the privilege to create, maintain and/or search databases. Thus one or more 'central' DBAs is unavoidable.

STATUS Suitable for use either centrally or for an individual's
textbases. There is no need for a central DBA. Each textbase needs
one or more identified managers.

- The activities associated with the DBA role require a number of
tools. Many of these are the subject of detailed comment in other
sections, but it is worth noting here that these tools should, in
general, be provided in a consistent way and not as a collection of
ad hoc utilities each employing its own command style. *Comment
on consistency of DBA tools.*

BASIS DBA tools are an ad hoc collection of utilities, with more or less
consistent sets of parameters. Relevant ones have been mentioned
under appropriate trigger elsewhere.

BRS/Search BRS/Search programs have a consistent user interface -
following the usual UNIX command format. Many of the tools
required by the DBA however are available via the usual
menu-driven interface.

STATUS Generally they are a collection of utilities accessible from VMS
with a consistent user image. Some such as RECOVER are accessed
from STATUS commands.

Summary of Section 6.8 It is **important** that adequate mechanisms
are provided for the control of the database. BRS/Search requires
that at least one, central DBA is required while the DBA tools
provided by BASIS are less than ideal.

6.9   System monitoring

6.9.1   Statistics

It should be easy to obtain performance statistics access times, retrieval
time, database usage, file and index sizes etc. *Comment on availability of
these in* logged *[not just on-the-fly] form.*

BASIS Some may be gleaned from the monitor file, and from most utilities,
but nothing specific. Release L includes a system performance monitor
utility.

BRS/Search Not extensive. The sizes of all files involved can be easily obtained via the BRSSIZE program. A user can also easily find out what databases he has used and when. The database name, sign-on time and sign-off time (and duration) can easily be listed, as can off-line print statistics. System administrators can get a similar report for any user, group of users or all users (the same goes for databases). No log is kept of other system performance figures.

STATUS The manuals and a specific training course provide some advice on optimisation of database performance; there are no specific performance analysis tools.

6.9.2 Tuning

It should be possible to tune by e.g. altering indexing strategies, adding new indexes, repair or balancing indexes etc. Data should never need to be dumped and re-loaded purely for tuning purposes. *Comment on availability and power of tuning tools. If such tools exist, note whether re-load required.*

BASIS Few tuning features available as yet, though more are promised for Release L.

BRS/Search The load program BRSLOAD used with option -analyze will produce statistics and these can be used in a decision as to when to reorganise database files. If documents are only added to a database it should only be necessary to periodically reorganise the index files. If documents are also modified or deleted then the text files will also require reorganisation on occasions to retain efficiency. The BRSLOAD program with various options reorganises database files.

STATUS The Textbase Transfer programs provide tools for adding new indexes, repairing and balancing indexes, and merging and splitting textbases without reload.

6.9.3 Audit trail

It should be possible to maintain an audit trail of all access to databases, invisibly to users. *Note whether audit trail possible and whether transparent. Note availability of tools for analysis and report generation.*

BASIS If a monitorfile is in use, the MSTATS utility may be used to provide very detailed statistics about database usage, broken down by user, command type, document sets created etc.

BRS/Search In native mode only, a trail file can be obtained that will hold all keystrokes used in a search session. This could also be achieved in an MNS interface.

STATUS An audit trail feature has been made available to customers but is not at present part of the standard product. At the highest level it logs all textbase choices and times of change along with all commands used; it is transparent to users.

Summary of Section 6.9 It is **important** that adequate system monitoring facilities are provided. BRS/Search provides only limited access to performance statistics while BASIS scores on its ability to provide detailed usage statistics.

Chapter 7

General Considerations

This section discusses a range of issues in the assessment of software in general. As such it complements the previous discussion of issues specific to Free Text software.

7.1 Documentation

7.1.1 Printed documentation

Good user documentation is of the greatest importance. As a minimum the vendors should supply both a User Guide and a Reference Manual: the distinction being that the User Guide provides a narrative whereas the Reference Manual is looked-up for definitive entries on specific topics (typically commands). An introductory Training Manual is also useful. *Comment on the existence/quality of these three types of manual.*

BASIS The following are available:

- DBA Guide to BASIS (discursive detailed blow-by-blow account of how to design a database, aimed at professional DP person)
- DBA Topics Manual (more specific technical details of some topics)
- DBA Reference Manual (well organised exhaustive reference manual)

- Users Reference Manual (covers use of existing database exhaustively, but is incomprehensible to average user and very badly written)

- Programmers Reference Manual (good coverage of HLI and other system level interfaces: usable by programmers only)

- Utilities Manual (describes operating system interfaces and functionality of all utilities and commands, in all implementations: fairly impenetrable and mostly irrelevant to any user)

- Introduction to Basis (summarises most facilities, but rather out of date)

- Quick reference and pocket guides are available, but cover retrieval and limited updating facilities only.

Serious use will invariably require at least three and probably all manuals open on desk simultaneously. Conclusion: documentation not ideally structured.

BRS/Search The documentation set is contained in 3 A4-size ring binders and includes:

- User's Manual: User's Guide; Search Primer; Errors and Messages Guide

- System Administrator's Manual: Database Customisation Guide; Installation Configuration Environment Guide

- Technical Reference Manual: Print-time Formatting Guide; MNS Reference Guide; Thesaurus Use and Reference Guide

The Installation Configuration Environment Guide is system dependent. Versions exist for UNIX, VM/CMS, VMS and MS-DOS. A useful A5-size MS-DOS user manual also exists. New versions of the software are accompanied by release notes. A short Questions and Answers note gives a lot of useful facts about BRS/Search. There is no quick reference guide or pocket guide for the experienced user. The general quality of the documentation is good.

STATUS The following manuals are provided :

- Installing and Operating STATUS

- Planning, Creating and Administrating

- Transfer Programs

- Utilities

- Textbase Users Guide

- Command Reference Manual

For add-ons

- Data Preparation Aid
- Thesaurus Handler
- Report Generator

Both User Guide and Reference manual exist fulfilling the functions described. The User guide also provides a suggested learning script for training purposes. Some of the versions seen were in final draft with incomplete indexing. In general they are well produced and easily used. The present trend for a smaller, more easily carried, page format in many manuals has not been followed. There is no quick reference guide or pocket guide for the experienced user. The trend in documentation design is to provide more screen examples.

7.1.2 On-line help

On-line documentation is useful but secondary to the printed manuals. To be immediately useful to the user it must be integrated into a HELP system which can be searched by keyword and which is usually hierarchically structured. *Note whether on-line help available and whether it is context-sensitive.*

BASIS Adequate built in help for querying databases. (?COMMANDS lists all commands; ?*command* gives details on *command*). Can be fairly easily customised (in DDL). No help provided at all for standard utilities. No VMS Help library. Much of available help is redundant to a given implementation. Dialogue file can be customised to change language used, and all messages redefined to improve this.

BRS/Search There is extensive (context sensitive) online help available at any time in the provided menu-driven interfaces. In the native mode interface, ..WHAT COMMANDS with arguments DATABASES or PARAGRAPHS or OPERATORS or TERMINALS all supply useful prompting information. All the BRS/Search programs have an optional parameter (-help...a la UNIX) that describe the commands.

STATUS Available, not context sensitive. HELP *command-name*. The help in full screen query or display mode is better, more easily accessed and relevant to the screen context.

Summary of Section 7.1 It is **very important** in an academic environment, where many different levels of expertise may be expected, that there is comprehensive and comprehensible documentation on the facilities that are available. All three systems provide documentation materials for a range of uses, e.g., for the professional DBA when setting up a database or for an inexperienced user while carrying out a search. There is little to choose between the systems in the case of the printed documentation but BRS/Search scores in the range of context-sensitive information that is available online.

7.2 Vendor Support

7.2.1 Organisation

The supporting organisation should be based in this country, be of reasonable size and financial security and, in general, be able to offer credible promises of continuity of service. An independent UK user group, regularly consulted by the vendor, is also desirable. *Comment on supporting organisation. Note whether user group is active in UK.*

BASIS Information Dimensions (Europe) is based in Geneva; Information Dimensions (UK) based in London; very active product development, which appears highly responsive to user input; active and enthusiastic user group with regular meetings.

BRS/Search The package was introduced in 1982. BRS-Europe based in London started trading in 1983 and the system is now in wide use in Europe and the USA. At the end of 1988, BRS-Europe, along with BRS Inc in the USA, were bought by Robert Maxwell. There is an active European User group, not a UK one. Annual meetings generally attract a hundred or so participants.

STATUS HCP is a UK company financed by UKAEA, Rothschilds and Computer Power (Australia). There is an active independent User Group which holds two conferences per year in the UK.

7.2.2 Updates

There should be new releases of the software at relatively frequent intervals: if, say, more than two years elapses between releases then it is likely that the vendors have started to drift and the product is not being

properly maintained. It will certainly be falling behind the opposition.
Note number of major releases in last five years.

BASIS Major releases annual over last three years at least.

BRS/Search BRS-Europe say that there have been 4 major releases of the
software in the past 5 years. The aim is for 1 per year, but in reality this
is more like 15 months. intermediate releases are provided for some
operating systems, generally to cope with a change to the operating
system or C compiler (VMS was mentioned here).

STATUS Four - last in early to mid 1988 so far available on limited range of
operating systems which includes MVS/TSO, VM/CMS, VMS, MSDOS,
UNIX, Wang VS. Others including UNIX System V and Prime available
from April 1989.

7.2.3 Documentation

The documentation should be maintained in step with the software.
Although it is unreasonable to expect every change (which may simply be
bug fixes) to be accompanied by new issues of the documentation, every
major release must be accompanied by appropriate new documentation.
Note whether each major release accompanied by revised documentation.

BASIS Documentation has been restructured at each of last three major
releases. Updates are also issued for minor changes and corrections.

BRS/Search The documentation is kept in step with the new releases either
by issuing an update to an existing document, or by re-issuing a new set.

STATUS Yes, always.

Summary of Section 7.2 It is clearly **important** in the case of a bulk
purchase agreement that the academic community has confidence in
the organisation that is providing the software and in its ability to
maintain and enhance the basic product. All three packages
considered here have a high reputation in the market place;
however, Information Dimensions, the vendors of BASIS, is felt to
have a slight edge over the other two vendors in terms of its size,
organisational stability and (over BRS/Search) in having an active
UK-based user group.

7.3   Costs

1. Exact costs should be provided for the following:-

   - The package in the first year
   - Documentation (how many copies? user photocopying allowed?)
   - Annual maintenance
   - Subsequent years' rental

   Costs should be specified both at the standard commercial rate, and after application of any available academic discount.

2. The charging basis (whether by site/installation or by processing node) should be clearly specified.

3. Any effect of discount terms on the level of support should be clearly specified.

4. It is important to be clear whether new releases of the software and the documentation are available automatically or whether they come on payment of extra fees. Bug-fixing issues must be automatically available. *Describe pricing structure.*

   BASIS Updates are included in maintenance charge (which also covers extensive software support and advice from the telephone HotLine)

   BRS/Search The annual maintenance charge covers new releases of the software and provides for telephone support.

   STATUS New releases and bug fixes are included in the annual maintenance charges, and are made available at no extra cost.

Summary of Section 7.3 *The material in this section was covered in a separate description which we do not reproduce here. It was the result of negotiations carried out on behalf of the Working Party by the Combined Higher Education Software Team (CHEST), based at Bath University.*

7.4   Installation

Any requirements of the product for other software, such as a particular compiler or operating system, should be noted. If the source code is available, it should be in a standard version of a standard language. Some indication of the amount of time and expertise required to mount the software should be obtained. *Comment on any major installation issues. Note particularly what other software, such as compilers or special operating system features, is required.*

BASIS Software is very easily installed in a VAX VMS environment, and seems to have no dependencies, other than use of VMS sort utility. All IO and other low-level functions performed by supplied BASLIB library. Current release was tested under both VMS4 and VMS5 without incident.

BRS/Search The C version of BRS/Search (used to be called the mini/micro version), is the version running on all but the large IBM mainframes and is written entirely in C. The presence of a C compiler is not necessary however. The source could be made available to any site that enters an agreement to port to a new environment. The source is not normally distributed.

STATUS Easily installed on a Vax CI Cluster under VMS. No dependencies observed. Not able to test STATUS E under VMS versions other than 4.6 and 4.7a, but customers are using VMS 5 now. HCP say that under IBM TSO or CMS Fortran run time libraries are needed to use the report writing add-on.

Summary of Section 7.4 *The summary for this Section appears with that for the next Section, below.*

7.5   Hardware

7.5.1   Devices

The product may be able to take advantage of special devices such as as light-pens, colour graphics, or exotic printers. Such features should not however be prerequisites for any use of the software. *Note any exotic devices supported and whether required for system to run.*

BASIS None needed.

BRS/Search No exotic devices are needed. BRS/Search has been used for databases published on CD-ROM. Terminal and printer characteristics can be defined and utilised to enhance displays and printed output.

STATUS None needed, but can support light pens and colour graphic devices. In addition it is being used in certain projects in conjunction with CD-Roms and WORM devices holding both text and graphical information. It has been interfaced with image scanners for image processing systems and text scanners for direct input as marked-up STATUS documents.

7.5.2   Configuration

The minimum configuration on which the product will run (processor, memory and disc) should be clearly stated. *Note whether such information available. If values seem remarkable, remark on them.*

BASIS Can be run on MicroVAX. Needs 512K memory, 25 Mb of disk for system. Users require open file quota of at least 40, subprocess quota of at least 2, BYTLM of 8192, ENQLM of at least 20. The executable code requires approximately 7 Mb of disc storage, and the object modules require 13.5 Mb.

BRS/Search Reflecting its UNIX background, BRS/Search is keen on spawning subprocesses. Under VMS a minimum value of 6 is necessary, 10 is preferred. The only other quotas that may need increasing are BYTLM (to 16384, although 8192 is adequate for a search-only user) and PGFLQUO (to 12800). Nothing else is out of the ordinary. A minimum of 7000 VMS blocks (1 block is 512k bytes) is recommended for the system. Under VMS the BRS/Search system manager would likely need a few quotas increased.

STATUS Supplied for Vax on 1600 bpi magnetic tape or TK50. Installation requires 17000 free disc blocks. The full screen version of STATUS requires VT series terminal under VMS and assigns keypad keys. A user session requires creation of spill file as a scratch file extended in units of 50 blocks. A private macro file resides in the user's login file and occupies at least 100 blocks. No recommendation for user VMS quotas; we have operated successfully with our system defaults.

Discuss microcomputer version, if any. Note major differences from standard product

BASIS No version currently available for machines smaller than a MicroVAX. The searching component of the system has been packaged with CD-ROM publications.

BRS/Search The version of BRS/Search running under MS-DOS on IBM PC-XT and compatibles is a single process implementation. Therefore no multi-tasking, queues, etc can be supported and database loading and printing cannot be carried out as a background process. The presently released version for MS-DOS is Version 3 of the software, but work is in progress bringing it up to Version 4. Most of the functionality of the multi-process C version is retained. It is supplied with the Searchmate and Eagle interfaces as standard, but MNS and Print-time formatting are available and so other interfaces can be written. System requirements are: an IBM PC XT-type computer with 512k memory and a hard disk (a 10 Mbyte one is sufficient for small databases). The system is supplied on four 320k byte disks, which includes some small test databases. The manual is only adequate, but the on-line help system is very useful.

STATUS The microcomputer version has exactly the same functionality as the VMS version with the exception of full screen query. Files can be transferred between micro and Vax versions in either direction without rebuild. Requires 512kb memory, 10 Mb hard disc and MSDOS 2.0 or later. A similar configuration is needed for Unix micros.

Summary of Sections 7.4 and 7.5 It is **very important** that the chosen system can be implemented with little difficulty in an academic computing environment and can be run on as wide a range of equipment as possible. All three packages score well here, but BASIS loses out by reason of the lack of a microcomputer version, the minimum hardware requirement being a microVAX.

Chapter 8

Conclusions

Each of the three packages considered here has a good reputation that has
been built up over several years and is now well-established in the market
place. Our extensive, comparative evaluation has shown that all of these
reputations are very well-deserved; indeed, it is worth noting that it was
not possible to differentiate between the three of them in no less than 38
of the 70 comparative tests which we carried out. Thus, ANY of these
packages can be expected to give an excellent level of performance. The
reader should note that, while we have been able to make an overall
recommendation, this is specific to our particular application context,
that of the higher education market, and different environments might
well have different requirements leading to an alternative final choice. A
further problem is that it is difficult to reconcile the many performance
comparisons which we have carried out since the tests relate to very
different features of the software; in making an overall recommendation,
we thus run the inevitable risk of adding apples and pears to get an
overall ranking based on oranges.

Bearing these points in mind, our overall evaluation of the three packages
is as follows:

BASIS This is an exceedingly comprehensive package that allows the
user a very wide range of facilities, some of which are just not
available in the other two, e.g., the way in which it can handle the

Shakespeare data; however, this degree of flexibility means that the system is necessarily complex in operation in some cases. The two main limitations which we have identified are the rather forbidding user interface and the unsophisticated approach that has been adopted for proximity searching.

BRS/Search This is a well-rounded package which provides a good interface and excellent searching routines. The re-indexing capabilities are limited and we are not convinced of the effectiveness of the recovery facilities that are provided.

STATUS The most noticeable advantages of this package over the other two are the wide range of facilities for browsing in full text. It is available for some hardware platforms for which the other two do not currently have implementations. There are, however, several weaknesses, in particular the amount of work that is needed for data input, the non-standard way in which the Boolean retrieval sets are manipulated and the use of thesaural control only during searching.

Our final conclusion, based on the technical evidence above, is that both BASIS and BRS/Search do seem to have a significant advantage over STATUS when considered for use in an academic computing environment. We are not able to differentiate between BASIS and BRS/Search on the basis of the tests which we have carried out (and the choice of package for an individual organisation would be determined by which software features were most appropriate to their specific needs). This being so, the choice of the most recommendable package must take account of the financial offers which have been put forward by the package suppliers.

(The three package suppliers had been asked to state terms for the purchase of their product by the Higher Education community. In the light of these offers, BRS/Search was purchased for the community in early 1989, using funds made available by the Computer Board for Universities and Research Councils.)

Appendix A

Test Procedures

The following sub-sections give the details of individual test procedures which have been referred to in the main document.

A.1 The test data

A.1.1 Mail

This dataset consists of 117 electronic mail messages extracted from the Humanist Bulletin Board maintained at the University of Toronto. The messages were copied from the VAX/VMS mail system into a sequential file. Each message is prefixed by tagged fields indicating the sender (FROM) the date sent (DATE) the topic of the message (SUBJECT) and the text of the message itself (TEXT). Evaluators should describe how this test data set was loaded, specifying any pre-processing steps which were required.

BASIS The data needed only a minor edit (the space in front of the colons after the field prefixes had to be removed) before it was loaded using FREE.FORM.B. The linebreaks of the original were preserved because some of the messages relied on layout to convey information; alternatively the text of the messages could have been loaded in such a way that

BASIS would do word-wrapping automatically on display. This can only be changed by reloading the data.

BRS/Search The data as supplied was almost in a form that could be loaded into a suitably defined BRS database, but required some pre-processing to suit the definition that was planned for the database. In particular, the document boundary was edited to produce

```
*** BRS DOCUMENT BOUNDARY ***
```

followed by a line containing the field tag for the document number, which called Number : and the number. (Note that the document number was originally a part of the document boundary). A field tag for the body (text) of the message was produced also. Finally, the data in the date field was converted into numeric form to aid date searching. Note that the pre-processing above could be achieved with a simple filter. Three 'print time formats' were then defined that would deliver

1. a pretty format suitable for the application, displaying all relevant data

2. a summary format (one line per document) giving the primary key, document number, date and the first 20 or 30 characters of the sender and subject

3. a format that reproduced the original data format (as received via JANET MAIL).

The usual (BRS) default format was also available.

STATUS Two chapters were distinguished for demonstration purposes and these were separated by value of date sent An individual mail message is an article. Named sections were From, At (Location) and Subject Keyed fields were Date and Mail Number The main text forms one or more paragraphs. Extensive text marking was carried out in EDT to indicate to Status which text filled which field. An example is given in Figure A.1. The character '<' preserves a blank line or in other circumstances preserves the line structure.

A.1.2 Shakespeare

This dataset consists of the text of Shakespeare's play *Love's Labours Lost* extensively tagged for analysis by software such as the Oxford Concordance Program. This text was made available to the working party by the Oxford Text Archive, for the purposes of this evaluation only. Line format:

Figure A.1: STATUS : The mail dataset

```
$$T
$$N From
MCCARTY
$$N LOCATION
EARN.UTOREPAS
#DATE 25 January 1988   #MAILNO   362
$$T
$$N SUBJECT
The hypermedia bibliography reformatted (16 lines)
<
$$P
Sebastian Rahtz (cmi011@ibm.southampton.ac.uk, if you speak
Bitnet) has kindly put the hypermedia bibliography into BibTeX
format and promised to send it to anyone interested.
Please write to him directly rather than to me.
Yours, Willard McCarty
$$A
```

- Lines longer than 80 chars are indicated by a plus + in column 80

- Lines are given through-scene numbering, in columns 1-4 of each line

- Column 5 is used to indicate amphibious (A) or broken (B) verse lines

- Column 6 is always blank

Text format: Passages of editorial or other comment are enclosed in brackets [[and]]. Tags suitable for the Oxford Concordance Program (OCP) were embedded in the text to indicate the following features:

- <O number of following text i.e. order in Wells-Taylor ed

- <H short title of piece (used as filename)

- <D date of composition

- <K type of composition (play, verse etc)

- <A authorship

- <T type of text following (verse, prose, stage direction etc)

- <S speaker of following speech. Speech prefixes are listed at the end of each play

- <X major (act) divisions

- <Y minor (scene) division

Character usage:

- Upper and lowercase characters and numbers

- { ... } encloses passages in italics

- _ is used for an em-dash

- ' opens double quotes and " closes them

- accents are indicated by characters following the accented letter as follows:

  - / acute
  - \ grave
  - @ cedilla
  - | diaresis
  - ˜ tilde
  - ˆ circumflex

Evaluators should describe how this test data set was loaded, specifying any pre-processing steps which were required.

BASIS This dataset required some massaging to support all the functions required. In the first stage, the text was divided into speeches and tags for use by FORMS were introduced. Two new fields were added to every speech: one simply containing the line number/s and the other the type/s of text used in the speech (verse, prose, stage). Every point within the text where text-type changed was marked explicitly, as a new context unit, so that an appropriate link code would be generated for it in the index transaction file. This preprocessing was done by a simple Fortran program. The process is illustrated in Figures A.2 and A.3. This output was run through FORMS in the usual way. The index transactions generated from this data use the same indexing prefix for all parts of the text, but the link codes (the second column of numbers) change where the text type changes. By reference to the entries using the prefix TTYPE it is thus possible to replace the DATA prefix by the appropriate one of VERSE STAGE or PROSE. This was carried out by a second Fortran program, which processed the file of index transactions before loading them into the index. The process is illustrated in Figures A.4 and A.5. To support searching across text-type (i.e. anywhere in text), a mapped prefix is defined in the DDL.

BRS/Search It is not possible to construct the overlapping hierarchical structure that is necessary to properly support all the functions required here. Nevertheless, by introducing paragraph breaks after each speech that starts a line it is possible for a search to narrow the possible areas of interest using the word proximity function. With this in mind the input data was simply edited to introduce a blank line in between speeches that start a line. In this way the database was created seemingly only containing a number of paragraphs. With a little further preprocessing, Act, Scene and Line Numbers could have been added for each paragraph.

STATUS Each Act is a chapter and each scene is an article. Named sections were each individual speaker and stage directions which, for demonstration purposes were not concorded. No keyed fields but provision was left for later creation of some. Line numbers were concorded as normal text strings and the file processed with a program to insert '<' characters at the end of each line for display purposes. Space was left for an additional chapter which could contain a search guide. An example of the marked text is given in Figure A.6.

A.1.3 Homer

This dataset consists of the first six books of Homer's *Iliad*, transcribed according to the conventions used by the Thesaurus Linguae Graecae. The letters of the Greek alphabet are transliterated according to the scheme in Table A.1. The file is divided into six books, each prefixed by a book reference in the form <B n><L 1>. Each line of the input file represents a Greek verse line. There is no structural unit larger than a line but smaller than a book, and words of text are not tagged in any way. Requirements: Should be able to index in such a way that can retrieve words case/accent sensitive/blind. Ask suppliers to comment on how they would display using greek characters (a) on a PC emulating VT100 (b) on the output device they would recommend for the purpose. Would changes be needed in database if hardware changed? Evaluators should describe how this test data set was loaded, specifying any pre-processing steps which were required.

Figure A.2: BASIS : Preprocessing the Shakespeare dataset, first pass, input

```
127  <S BIRON> A dangerous law against gentility.
128  <T prose> 'Item: if any man be seen to talk with a woman
within
129  the term of three years, he shall endure such public
130  shame as the rest of the court can possible devise."
131  <T verse> This article, my liege, yourself must break;
132  For well you know here comes in embassy
133  The French King's daughter with yourself to speak_
134  A maid of grace and complete majesty_
135  About surrender-up of Aquitaine
136  To her decrepit, sick, and bedrid father.
137  Therefore this article is made in vain,
138  Or vainly comes th' admire\d Princess hither.
139  <S KING> What say you, lords? Why, this was quite forgot.
```

BASIS The OCP tags in the original source file were edited into a form suitable for input to FORMS using the VMS TPU utility. This is shown in Figure A.7. To support accent-blind searching in this text, the index file generated by FORMS was then processed by a simple Fortran program. This simply generated additional entries for any terms in the index which had the prefix TEXT and also contained accents. The additional entry had a different prefix (TEXTX) and the same term without accents. The process is illustrated in Figures A.8 and A.9.

BRS/Search The original file was edited in a very simple way for input into a BRS database. This is illustrated in Figure A.10. To support accent-blind and accent-sensitive searching in this text, it was decided to build two databases. In the definition of the database form for the accent blind database, the characters that were to be ignored when searching and which did not define word boundaries were defined in a 'noiselist'. These characters are however displayed when viewing or updating the text. The relevant portions of the form file are shown in Figure A.11. For the accent sensitive database a noiselist was not required, however the language used had to be redefined in order to support searching for the accent characters. The documentation in this area is apparently clear, but gives insufficient detail and a certain amount of trial and error was involved. The 'Greek' language table was constructed by editing the standard character set file, which is a small (11 line ASCII file) and then this was compiled with the BRSLANG utility. Two other files had to be created (by copying and editing existing files) in order to deal with the fact that some of the accent characters had meaning to BRS/Search. Thus, for

Figure A.3: BASIS : Preprocessing the Shakespeare dataset, first pass, output

```
FD:
FD:
ACT:1
SCENE:1
SPEAKER:BIRON
  127  <S BIRON> A dangerous law against gentility.
  128  %<T prose> 'Item: if any man be seen to talk with a woman
within
  129  the term of three years, he shall endure such public
  130  shame as the rest of the court can possible devise."
  131  %<T verse> This article, my liege, yourself must break;
  132  For well you know here comes in embassy
  133  The French King's daughter with yourself to speak_
  134  A maid of grace and complete majesty_
  135  About surrender-up of Aquitaine
  136  To her decrepit, sick, and bedrid father.
  137  Therefore this article is made in vain,
  138  Or vainly comes th' admire\d Princess hither.
TTYPE:X,p,v,
LINES:127,128,129,130,131,132,133,134,135,136,137,138,
FD:
FD:
ACT:1
SCENE:1
SPEAKER:KING
  139  <S KING> What say you, lords? Why, this was quite forgot.
TTYPE:v,
LINES:139,
```

Figure A.4: BASIS : Preprocessing the Shakespeare dataset, second pass, input

```
Sample input to SHAKITR:
      396255   4 I SPEAKER=BIRON
      396 2    6 I TTYPE=P
      396 3    6 I TTYPE=V
      396 1    6 I TTYPE=X
      396 1   20 I DATA=127
      396 1   20 I DATA=128
      396 2   20 I DATA=129
      396 2   20 I DATA=130
      ........
      396 3   20 I DATA=VAINLY
      396 3   20 I DATA=VERSE
      396 3   20 I DATA=WELL
      396 2   20 I DATA=WITH
      396 3   20 I DATA=WITH
      396 2   20 I DATA=WITHIN
      396 2   20 I DATA=WOMAN
      396 2   20 I DATA=YEARS
      396 3   20 I DATA=YOU
      396 3   20 I DATA=YOURSELF
      396 2   20 I DATA='ITEM
      396255   0 I ALL
      397255   4 I SPEAKER=KING
      397 1    6 I TTYPE=V
      397 1   20 I DATA=139
      397 1   20 I DATA=FORGOT
      397 1   20 I DATA=KING
      397 1   20 I DATA=LORDS
      397 1   20 I DATA=QUITE
      397 1   20 I DATA=S
      397 1   20 I DATA=SAY
      397 1   20 I DATA=THIS
      397 1   20 I DATA=WAS
      397 1   20 I DATA=WHAT
      397 1   20 I DATA=WHY
      397 1   20 I DATA=YOU
      397255   0 I ALL
```

Figure A.5: BASIS : Preprocessing the Shakespeare dataset, second pass, output

```
Sample output from SHAKITR:
      396255   4 I SPEAKER=BIRON
      396  2  20 I PROSE=129
      396  2  20 I PROSE=130
     . . . . . . . . . . .
      396  3  20 I VERSE=VAINLY
      396  3  20 I VERSE=VERSE
      396  3  20 I VERSE=WELL
      396  2  20 I PROSE=WITH
      396  3  20 I VERSE=WITH
      396  2  20 I PROSE=WITHIN
      396  2  20 I PROSE=WOMAN
      396  2  20 I PROSE=YEARS
      396  3  20 I VERSE=YOU
      396  3  20 I VERSE=YOURSELF
      396  2  20 I PROSE='ITEM
      396255   0 I ALL
      397255   4 I SPEAKER=KING
      397  1  20 I VERSE=139
      397  1  20 I VERSE=FORGOT
      397  1  20 I VERSE=KING
      397  1  20 I VERSE=LORDS
      397  1  20 I VERSE=QUITE
      397  1  20 I VERSE=S
      397  1  20 I VERSE=SAY
      397  1  20 I VERSE=THIS
      397  1  20 I VERSE=WAS
      397  1  20 I VERSE=WHAT
      397  1  20 I VERSE=WHY
      397  1  20 I VERSE=YOU
      397255   0 I ALL
```

Figure A.6: STATUS : The Shakespeare dataset

```
$$N BIRON
  127  A dangerous law against gentility.<
  128  <PROSE> 'Item: if any man be seen to talk with a woman within<
  129  the term of three years, he shall endure such public<
  130  shame as the rest of the court can possible devise."<
  131  <VERSE> This article, my liege, yourself must break;<
  132  For well you know here comes in embassy<
  133  The French King's daughter with yourself to speak_<
  134  A maid of grace and complete majesty_<
  135  About surrender-up of Aquitaine<
  136  To her decrepit, sick, and bedrid father.<
  137  Therefore this article is made in vain,<
  138  Or vainly comes th' admire\d Princess hither.<
$$N KING
  139  What say you, lords? Why, this was quite forgot.<
```

example, the use of curly brackets {} in place of round brackets (), which
are normally used to nest searches, had to be defined. (Round brackets
were two of the accent characters). In the database form file, the
alternative character set definition was specified, and no noise list was
present. The start of the form file in this case in shown in Figure A.12.

STATUS Each book formed a chapter and each sub division formed an article.
In practice this meant that at least one article lasted a whole book. No
named sections or keyed fields were defined. The file was processed with a
program to insert '<' character at the end of each line for display
purposes. Two versions of the textbase were developed to cope with
accent blind searching, one in which the non alphabetic characters were
ignored and another in which the index contained these characters. An
example of the marked text is given in Figure A.13.

A.1.4   MARC data

A tape containing about 500 records in standard UK MARC exchange
tape format was made available to the Working Party by the Oxford
University Libraries automation project. Manufacturers were asked to
comment on how they would extract from it the fields shown in Table A.2.
For the purposes of the evaluation, it will be necessary to extract the data
from the tape in a form which can be loaded directly into the system

Table A.1: Conventions for the Homer data set.

A a	alpha	punctuation used: -,.:_'"
B b	beta	
X x	xi	) smooth breathing
D d	delta	(rough breathing
E e	epsilon	/ acute ·
F f	phi	= circumflex
G g	gamma	\ grave
H h	eta	+ diaeresis
I i	iota	? subscript dot
K k	kappa	| iota subscript
L l	lambda	
M m	mu	
N n	nu	
O o	omikron	Accents are given AFTER lowercase
P p	pi	letters to which they apply, but
Q q	theta	BEFORE uppercase ones, as is
R r	rho	conventional. Up to 3 accents
S s	sigma	may appear on a single letter.
T t	tau	
U u	upsilon	
V	digamma	
W w	omega	
C c	chi	
Y y	psi	
Z z	zeta	

Figure A.7: BASIS : Preprocessing the Homer dataset, first pass
Input form:

```
<A HOMER>
<T ILIAD>
<B 1>
Mh=nin a)/eide, qea\, Phlhi+a/dew )Axilh=os
ou)lome/nhn, h(\ muri/' )Axaioi=s a)/lge' e)/qhke,
polla\s d' i)fqi/mous yuxa\s )/Ai+di proi/+ayen
h(rw/wn, au)tou\s de\ e(lw/ria teu=xe ku/nessin
...
```

Output form:

```
FD:
FD:
Author:HOMER
Title:ILIAD
Book:1
Mh=nin a)/eide, qea\, Phlhi+a/dew )Axilh=os
ou)lome/nhn, h(\ muri/' )Axaioi=s a)/lge' e)/qhke,
polla\s d' i)fqi/mous yuxa\s )/Ai+di proi/+ayen
h(rw/wn, au)tou\s de\ e(lw/ria teu=xe ku/nessin
...
```

Figure A.8: BASIS : Preprocessing the Homer dataset, second pass, input

```
1511  24 I AUTH=HOMER
1511  43 I TITLE=ILIAD
1511  44 I BOOK=1
1 60  71 I TEXT=(/HRH
1 36  71 I TEXT=(\WS
1 47  71 I TEXT=(\WS
1  3  71 I TEXT=)/AI+DI
1 32  71 I TEXT=)/ARGEI+
1 24  71 I TEXT=)/ENQ'
1 74  71 I TEXT=)/HTOI
1110  71 I TEXT=)/HTOI
1 77  71 I TEXT=)/ILION
1 97  71 I TEXT=)AGAME/MNONA
1 26  71 I TEXT=)AGAME/MNONI
1102  71 I TEXT=)AGAME/MNWN
1111  71 I TEXT=)AGAME/MNWN
1141  71 I TEXT=)AGAME/MNWN
1185  71 I TEXT=)AGAME/MNWN
1 47  71 I TEXT=)APO/LLWN
1 69  71 I TEXT=)APO/LLWN
1 78  71 I TEXT=)APO/LLWN
1 22  71 I TEXT=)APO/LLWNA
1 93  71 I TEXT=)APO/LLWNA
1 39  71 I TEXT=)APO/LLWNI
1 15  71 I TEXT=)APO/LLWNOS
```

Figure A.9: BASIS : Preprocessing the Homer dataset, second pass, output

```
1511   24  I  AUTH=HOMER
1511   43  I  TITLE=ILIAD
1511   44  I  BOOK=1
1 60   71  I  TEXT=(/HRH
1 60   71  I  TEXTX=HRH
1 36   71  I  TEXT=(\WS
1 36   71  I  TEXTX=WS
1 47   71  I  TEXT=(\WS
1 47   71  I  TEXTX=WS
1  3   71  I  TEXT=)/AI+DI
1  3   71  I  TEXTX=AIDI
1 32   71  I  TEXT=)/ARGEI+
1 32   71  I  TEXTX=ARGEI
1 24   71  I  TEXT=)/ENQ'
1 24   71  I  TEXTX=ENQ'
1 74   71  I  TEXT=)/HTOI
1 74   71  I  TEXTX=HTOI
1110   71  I  TEXT=)/HTOI
1110   71  I  TEXTX=HTOI
1 77   71  I  TEXT=)/ILION
1 77   71  I  TEXTX=ILION
1 97   71  I  TEXT=)AGAME/MNONA
1 97   71  I  TEXTX=AGAMEMNONA
1 26   71  I  TEXT=)AGAME/MNONI
1 26   71  I  TEXTX=AGAMEMNONI
1102   71  I  TEXT=)AGAME/MNWN
1102   71  I  TEXTX=AGAMEMNWN
1111   71  I  TEXT=)AGAME/MNWN
1111   71  I  TEXTX=AGAMEMNWN
1141   71  I  TEXT=)AGAME/MNWN
1141   71  I  TEXTX=AGAMEMNWN
1185   71  I  TEXT=)AGAME/MNWN
1185   71  I  TEXTX=AGAMEMNWN
1 47   71  I  TEXT=)APO/LLWN
1 47   71  I  TEXTX=APOLLWN
1 69   71  I  TEXT=)APO/LLWN
1 69   71  I  TEXTX=APOLLWN
```

Figure A.10: BRS : Preprocessing the Homer dataset, first pass

```
Input form:
<A HOMER>
<T ILIAD>
<B 1>
Mh=nin a)/eide, qea\, Phlhi+a/dew )Axilh=os
ou)lome/nhn, h(\ muri/' )Axaioi=s a)/lge' e)/qhke,
...
Output form:
<A HOMER
<T ILIAD
<B 1
<V
Mh=nin a)/eide, qea\, Phlhi+a/dew )Axilh=os
ou)lome/nhn, h(\ muri/' )Axaioi=s a)/lge' e)/qhke,
...
```

Figure A.11: BRS : Homer dataset, accent-blind version

```
\~
\~ Form File for Database HMEX
\~
            banner: IUSC FTWP Homer Greek Accent Blind Database
   .
   .
   .
noiselist:
")"
"("
"/"
       "\"
"="
"+"
"?"
"|"
:end
   .
   .
   .
```

Figure A.12: BRS : Homer dataset, accent-sensitive version

```
\~
\~ Form File for Database HMER
\~
            banner:
IUSC FTWP Homer Greek Accent Sensitive Database
         characterset: GREEK
    .
    .
    .
```

Figure A.13: STATUS: The Homer dataset

```
$$T
BOOK 1<
$$T
<
$$P
Mh=nin a)/eide, qea\, Phlhi+a/dew )Axilh=os<
ou)lome/nhn, h(\ muri/' )Axaioi=s a)/lge' e)/qhke,<
```

concerned, to define a database in which the above fields are all
searchable, and to load the data in. Not all of the above fields (which are
chosen more or less at random from those specified in the BLAISE-LINE
manual) are necessarily present in the supplied data: a useful side effect of
the extraction process would be a count of the number of occurrences of
each field in the first 500 records on the supplied MARC tape. Evaluators
should describe how this test data set was loaded, specifying any
pre-processing steps which were required.

BASIS The MARC data was converted to a format loadable into BASIS by a
utility provided by Information Dimensions (UK). The utility allowed
extraction of a subset of MARC fields (identified by tag) and their
mapping to user specified BASIS prefixes. The product currently
marketed by Information Dimensions operates on data conforming to the
US MARC standard; this conversion was done for the working party using
a similar system customised to handle UK MARC formats.

BRS/Search The MARC dataset was the only one of the four that required
BRS-Europe to provide any pre-processing program. To preprocess the
data they wrote a C program. The executable image, the input data and
all the database files were supplied by BRS-Europe on a VMS BACKUP
magnetic tape and were simply moved into the appropriate directories.

Table A.2: MARC fields

Prefix	Description	MARC tag
RCN	Record control number	001
IC	Information codes	008
LA	Languages	041
LC	Library Congress class number	050
DC	Dewey class number	082
AP	Personal name, main entry	100
TI	Title & statement responsibility	245
PA	Part title	248
PU	Imprint	260
PH	Collation	300
PI	Price/CIP status	350
N00-56	Notes	500-556
	(it should be possible to search for a specific note tag e.g. N46 or for any note)	
SH	Lib Congress Subject Heading	650
EP	Added Personal Name	700
GA	Geographic area code	043
PC	Corporate name series	810
RT	Title reference	945
SE	Series title	490
ED	Edition	250

STATUS Routines to handle the Marc data from tape were specially prepared for the exercise. Cobol programs were used to selectively bring down the data from tape in an understandable sequence and to convert this to Status input format. All fields were defined as concorded named sections, some of which occurred more than once in a record. An example is given in Figure A.14.

Figure A.14: STATUS : The MARC dataset

```
$$T
$$N TITLE
Quantum field theory and quantum statistics<
essays in honour of the sixtieth birthday of E.S. Fredkin<
$$T
$$N RECNO
#RECNO=b8622493
$$N INFOCODE
0512s1987     en ac   W     00111   eng b
$$N LC_CLASS
QC174.45
$$N DD_CLASS
530.1
$$N IMPRINT
Bristol Hilger c1987
$$N COLLATION
2 v. ill 2ports 24cm
$$N PRICE
No price : CIP rev.
$$N NOTES
504  Includes bibliographies and index
$$N NOTES
505  Contents: v.1 Quantum statistics - v.2. Models<
of field theory
$$N LC_SUBJECT
Quantum field theory
$$N ADDED_NAME
Fradkin
$$N ADDED_NAME
Batalin
$$N ADDED_NAME
Isham
$$N ADDED_NAME
Vilkovisky
$$A
```

A.2 Customised interfaces

Facilities should be provided to allow the creation of variant screen formats, tailored to the particular application and also to the level of user (context-sensitive). In particular, it must be possible to develop menu-driven interfaces rapidly and simply and to update these online if required. Evaluators should comment on

- the range of tools which is available

- level of support needed for their use, i.e, are they restricted to implementors or are they sufficiently well designed to allow users to create interfaces for themselves

- ease of use of the resulting screens, e.g., is it possible to opt out without having to traverse an entire hierarchy of menus

- are there varying levels of online help support provided, e.g., expert user, some experience, novice

Evaluators should attempt to create menus to

- input a new record into the test files

- carry out a simple query input, Boolean search and display (with extra marks if the Boolean structure can be hidden away from the user).

The results of these tests are given in Chapter 5.2, above.

A.3 Calling into the package

General Comment on quality of documentation of programming interface. General evaluative comment on richness of facilities offered and on the modularity of the software.

Basic test Write main program (in FORTRAN or a comparable high-level language) which passes to the package under test (using the conventions specified) the name of a field, a string to be searched-for in that field and the address of an integer variable to contain the number of hits in the data, and which prints the value of the integer variable on return from the package. Compile the program and attempt to link and run it: comment on results.

Refinement of basic test Revise program of basic test, above, to solve the same query by *direct inspection* of dictionary. Compile, etc: comment on results.

The results of these tests are given in Chapter 5.3.1, above.

A.4   Calling out from the package

Write FORTRAN subroutine (or equivalent in a comparable high-level language) which displays the text "Hello" on a suitable output device, such as a VDU. Using the conventions of the package under test, attempt to call the subroutine

- at all
- once per hit during a search.

If this second experiment is successful, rewrite the call and the subroutine to pass a string *from the data*, e.g. an item from the context in which the hit took place, and to print the string. Comment on results.

The results of these tests are given in Chapter 5.3.2, above.

A.5   Access to dictionary

Some indication should be obtained of the actions necessary to change the structure of an existing database and the effects of such changes on existing documents. For each of the following itemised changes, note whether the change is

- possible at all
- possible by rebuilding an index
- possible by rebuilding index and changing data in situ
- possible only by deleting and reloading data

Note what steps are needed to add a new field

- without affecting existing documents at all
- inserting a default value for the new field in existing documents
- inserting a value derived from existing data for the new field in existing documents

Note what steps are needed to change the definition of an existing field as follows:

- change its name or add a synonym
- increase its length
- decrease its length
- change its datatype (e.g. from string to integer)
- change from indexed to unindexed, or vice verse
- change the validation rules (e.g. to permit nulls, change valid range)
- apply or remove thesaurus control of terminology

In each of the above cases, indicate what steps would be necessary to make existing documents consistent with the new definitions.

The results of these tests are given in Chapter 6.1.1, above.

A.6 Indexing

- for MARC data: build one index on keywords and another on titles

- for email: build one index on senders of messages, on date and on topic & message independently and together.

- for Homer: index the text in such a way as to permit searching accent-blind or accent sensitive. In the first mode a search for a term will regard as hits any terms differing only from the search term with respect to the presence of accents (and any accents in the search term are ignored); in the second mode, any accents in the search term are significant.

- for Shakespeare: index the text in such a way as to permit searches to distinguish terms in any part of the text, terms categorised as prose, verse or stage-direction, and terms in speeches of a given speaker. It should be possible to combine these distinctions in a meaningful way, e.g. to recover all prose speeches of Armado in which the word "Honour" appears. The text should also be indexed by location (act, scene, line number), so that searches of the first kind can be constrained to a particular part of the play. It should also be possible to restrict such searches to italicised (or non-italicised) words. The cost (in terms of space and maintenance effort) of varying indexing strategies to support the full range of these facilities should be indicated.

The results of these tests are given in Chapter 6.1.3, above.

A.7 Thesaurus facilities

A small thesaurus was developed by the Working Party for the Mail dataset. A number of terms in the hierarchy participate in preferred and/or related term relations. The thesaurus was intended to allow the investigation of the following points:

A.7.1 Administrator functions

- the ease with which the thesaurus relations can be created and updated, e.g. by bulk loading

- whether the thesaurus is active or passive

- if active, what the effects on the dictionary and database are of changes to the thesaurus (c.f. A.5 above)

- if active, whether it may temporarily be disabled by the administrator and/or user

- whether a thesaurus may be declared specific to nominated fields

- whether more than one thesaurus may be invoked for a given data base

- whether the thesaurus browsing facilities are adequate for administrative and diagnostic purposes

The results of these tests are given in Chapter 6.4, above.

A.7.2 User functions

Formulate a number of queries using terms known to be contained in one or a number of thesaurus relations. Use thesaurus browsing facility to identify some candidate terms. Comment on the following,

- the ability to invoke a specific thesaurus for augmenting queries

- the ability to nominate a specific relation in order to expand the terms to be included in a query

- in the case of a hierarchic relation, the ability to limit the number of levels to be incorporated in any expansion of a term list

- the ability to browse through thesaurus relations and incorporate encountered terms in an augmented query

The results of these tests are given in Chapter 6.4, above.

A.8   Term searching

The software should be capable of searches for individual term
occurrences and for reasonably complex combinations of terms,
constrained in a large variety of ways. It should have a good pattern
matching capability. The user should be able to specify a search in terms
of Boolean expressions or a simplified version thereof. When searching for
terms of a particular category (or in a particular field), the user should be
able to specify at least the following as target:

- Simple term *eg* `FISH`

- Term *and* term *eg* `FISH` and `CHIPS` in the same context

- Term *before* term *eg* any `FISH` preceding `CHIPS`

- Term *after* term *eg* any `FISH` following `CHIPS`

- Terms separated by <n or >n or exactly 0 other terms *eg* `FISH` with
  1, 2, 3 etc words separating it from `CHIPS`

- Term *or* term *eg* either `FISH` or `CHIPS`

- Term *without* term *eg* all `FISH` not associated with `CHIPS`

The user should be able to specify matches as

- exact *eg* `FISH` but not `fish` or `Fish`

- case insensitive *eg* `FISH`, `fish` or `Fish` etc

- accent blind *eg* `Fi-sh` or `Fish` or `Fi\sh`

- involving a pattern built up from elements matching

    - 0 to n characters
    - exactly 1 character
    - any one of a specified set of characters

  eg `F*SH` to match `Fish`, `Fush`, `Flash`, `FSH`, `Farsh` etc ; `F?SH` to
  match `Fish` or `Fush` or `Fash` or `Fesh` or... ; `F[a,e]sh` to match `Fash`
  or `Fesh` and combinations thereof

- (where appropriate) involving the usual arithmetic comparisons (`GE GT LE LT EQ NE`); also range testing (*eg* between n and m)

The user should be able to specify the context within which a search involving more than one term is to be evaluated (e.g. same context unit, same field, same document, within some defined number of terms). Search conditions as specified above should be combinable within reasonable limits using `AND OR NOT` and bracketting as necessary to avoid ambiguity. Bracketting should be allowed to a depth of at least 20 levels, and the maximum number of terms permitted in an expression should be at least 75. It is also desirable to be able to specify a weighting to be attached to a particular condition and also to specify a quorum condition (i.e. count as a hit if more than some number of conditions has been satisfied, irrespective of which conditions they are).

The results of these tests are given in Chapter 6.2.1, above.

A.9   User-specified macros and SDI

Facilities should be available to allow users to define sequences of commands for subsequent execution. It is especially desirable that the command language for this should not be so intimidating as to inhibit the use of such facilities by relatively inexperienced users. Evaluators should identify some relatively simple sequence of commands and create a macro for execution; the following is suggested to evaluators:

- Exclusive OR, i.e., (A OR B) AND NOT (A AND B).

- Quorum search. Take a set of 5-6 query words and then generate all combinations of some user-defined number of terms, e.g., retrieve all documents having at least 3 terms in common with the query. Attempt to arrange things so that the macro can warn the user if an unacceptable number of combinations is going to be generated.

The system should provide facilities for SDI (Selective Dissemination of Information), i.e., the storage of predefined queries for running at a regular interval as new documents are added into the database; ideally, only the new documents are should be processed, not the entire database. Try to set up a simple profile for use with the mail test data set, e.g., keep people informed of anything to do with workstations or CAD. Load half of the file and then try to execute the stored questions as the second half of the file is loaded.

The results of these tests are given in Chapter 6.2.4, above.

Appendix B

Reference Sites

Each supplier was asked to provide the name of a contact at a customer site at which the relevant product had been in use for a reasonable time. A telephone interview with the contact was then held. The results are presented below, by package.

B.1 BASIS

Name of Site British Petroleum

Address BP International, Britannic House, Moor Lane, London EC2Y

Contact Person Duncan MacLean

Telephone Number 01-920 3964

Contactability The contact is moving on, but states that his successor should be approachable.

Time of Ownership BP have had BASIS in use since 1980, and the company now has about 20 licences.

Applications They have 100-150 applications, on both VAX and IBM platforms. About 1,000 staff regularly use them, with another 3,000 occasional users.

The largest database is about 500,000 records, 100,000 records is a common size, and the smallest have about 5,000. A group of about 8-16 staff provide an internal information centre service, and most of these staff are familiar with BASIS.

BP have developed their own 'BASIS environment', which they use for each new application. This includes facilities for data input.

Updating All updates are run overnight automatically from BASIS's queue file. Data is added to this by users during daytime. Users are allowed to preempt an overnight update, and update a database during the day, but as to do this would lock out other users during the update (which is not a quick event), this is not common. The software has never been known to corrupt a database.

BP recommend that each database has an administrator who checks the log file from update operations, this is most needed for databases containing numerical data, where 'range-errors', which are not trapped in quite the best way, may need correction.

Data Preparation Most is done online. On the VAX a front-end is used which accesses the queue file directly. Alternatively, word-processors on PCs are used to prepare data which is moved to the queue file.

Backups Normal VAX procedure are employed, with the addition that the queue file is backed to another disk drive before updating starts.

Opinions on Software When obtained in 1980, attempts were made to use it for quasi-relational tasks, but with the deployment of Ingres and Oracle within BP, BASIS is now employed for data which is mainly textual. It is felt to be a very good product in this area.

Its strengths were stated to be very fast and powerful retrieval capability, and the ability to build menu-driven front-ends.

Its weaknesses were felt to lie in its inability to perform relational data operations. Neither Olive nor the screen module were thought well of, indeed their perceived shortcomings had led to the development of the 'BASIS environment'.

Application-building was stated to be easy and quick, provided that the application itself was amenable. New applications could be put together quickly, using the definition-file from a previous one.

Quality and Service Issues BP thought BASIS was an excellent and stable product.

Its utilities were thought to be good.

Documentation used to be indifferent, but at the last version, it improved greatly.

Courses were stated to be very good, and were used regularly. End-users as well as information-centre staff attended them. They had become topic-oriented, so that people could be sent as and when a need for a particular skill arose.

Online help information was not reported to be great.

The support desk at Information Dimensions was not felt to be all that it might be, though it had improved considerably in the last year. Escalation of problems via Geneva to USA had been slow.

The User Group had in the past been rather run by the supplier, but the UK one was becoming more effective and independent. The European one was French-oriented.

Value for Money BP thought BASIS was a good product, and well worth its cost. They claimed to have looked around the marketplace about 3 years ago, and concluded that BASIS was worth staying with.

B.2 BRS/Search

Name of Site Peat, Marwick, McLintock

Address PO Box 486, 1 Puddle Dock, Blackfriars, London EC4V 3PD

Contact Person Nick Dimant

Telephone Number 01-236 8000 extension 7305

Contactability The contact was happy to answer questions from prospective purchasers.

Time of Ownership BRS/Search had been in use for about 18 months on a Microvax II and a VAX 11/780

Applications The software was bought for one main application, a database describing projects performed for their clients. The records contain breakdowns of the work done, with a textual summary. When tendering for consultancy, records are pulled from the database, sensitive information is edited automatically using the run-time print format features of BRS/Search, and a report for the prospective client is produced. Another database, of consultants' CVs (about six CVs per consultant, with about 600 consultants) is now being built. It will be used to generate information for tendering work.

About 600 users would be using the main application from early next year. The data comprised about 10Mb of text, in about 6,500 records.

Updating Updates were performed in batch runs. The database can be used while these are in progress (this was one of the factors that led PMM to choose BRS/Search). If an update were to fail, the database is believed to be left in a consistent state. No problems have been experienced in practice in this area. About 1,000 modest-sized records can be added in an hour. The package performs its own checkpoints during an update.

Data Preparation The Demon editor within BRS/Search was used here. It was good for data validation, and expansion of abbreviations. BRS/Search had integrated Wordperfect with the package for PMM, facilitating input of large text records in a textbase of consultants' CVs. For this work, standard facilities of BRS/Search had been employed to filter out markup codes from the WP output, and transform it to data for the free-text system. Data could be moved in either direction, allowing use of Wordperfect for document revision.

Backups On a nightly basis, incremental backups were alternated with full database dumps (possible with the modest volumes of data in use).

Opinions on Software The software was felt to be very good at handling textual data. The strengths of BRS/Search were felt to lie in text searching with versatility and precision, with more facilities being provided as standard than with other packages. The ability to configure an application by setting 'switches' (by the DBA or a user) was liked, as was the ability to define print-time formats for output.

The package was felt to be weak in its treatment of numeric data and the production of reports. For this work, PMM moved output from BRS/Search to other software, including Lotus and Oracle.

Quality and Service Issues The software itself was felt to be very good, as were the utilities.

The documentation, in two main manuals, was stated to be good.

Courses run by BRS/Search for both system-administrators and users were used, and were stated to be very good. They were given by technical staff who knew the software very well.

The online help provided by the package was not felt to be particularly good.

The support desk was praised as excellent.

The user group covered Europe as a whole, and was not felt to be particularly effective. There had been a UK one, but it had atrophied.

Value for Money The software was felt to represent good value for money.

B.3   STATUS

Name of Site Bank of England

Address Archive Section, Bank of England, Threadneedle Street, London EC2R 8AH

Contact Person Henry Gillet

Telephone Number 01-601 4889

Contactability The contact was happy to answer questions from prospective purchasers.

Time of Ownership STATUS had been in use for two years. STATUS/E was currently in use.

Applications One large and two smaller applications were supported. The main application concerned descriptions of archival records, which could range from simple to complex. About eight people used the package regularly. The main database comprised about 11Mb of text (plus indexes), in about 25,000 articles. Initially the application was run on a PC, but it migrated to a Microvax in June 1988.

Updating Updating is 'fairly undisciplined', but works well. New material is batched up, for 2 - 4 weeks, and then applied to the textbase. Small changes to existing articles are performed on the live database.

Data Preparation Data is collected on a word-processor on the PC, then put through a small conversion program which adds markup. It is then moved to the Microvax using Kermit, and kept for later addition.

Backups Backups to tape are performed every time data is added, and at weekends.

Opinions on Software The Bank were very pleased with their choice of STATUS. Its strengths were felt to lie in the ability to handle a very wide range of record structures, as some archive records really represented collections of simple items, and could be complex. Also liked were the macro language and the ability to route output from a search to designated files. Some complex macros which performed more than one enquiry were in use, the complexity being hidden from the user.

Three weaknesses were mentioned. Firstly the contents of macros could become complex (not uncommon!). Next, the processing time on keyed fields was frequently long, as as serial processing of the data was believed to be employed. Lastly, database loading was observed to be a very slow process.

As a vehicle for application-building, STATUS was felt to be good, though it was stated that the means of doing so was not particularly modern.

Quality and Service Issues STATUS was felt to be good package, though it was felt to be a little unfriendly.

The utilities were felt to be good, but they were too many in number and tend to be low-level. The wish was expressed that the package could operate more intelligently to occasion fewer runs of some utilities, such as the one used to compress a database.

Documentation was felt to be adequate, and that for STATUS/E was an improvement on previous provision.

The courses run by the software suppliers had been used for training, and were felt to be good, and well-paced. It was pointed out that after some reorganisation, Harwell Computer Power no longer run the courses, and that they were now contracted out.

Online help was stated to be adequate, but not impressive. The right questions had to be asked.

The support desk was stated to be helpful, and was used regularly. The desk does get back promptly, and bugs are fixed. The customer had a high opinion of the support given.

The user group was not felt to have much role, and its meetings were no longer attended.

Value for Money The package was felt to be good value for money.

Appendix C

Other Systems

This Appendix discusses systems which were not considered further after a preliminary analysis.

ASSASSIN A suitable package in many respects but suffering from the following disadvantages:

- Limited portability as only definitely available for ICL 2900 and Series 39, VMS and DOS/VSE/CICS.
- Unsatisfactory integration with other software. CALL IN and CALL OUT can be done but individual program modules are not available to the user. Links to other editors can only be made with the assistance of the ASSASSIN team.

CAIRS A competent package but with some deficiencies. Particular weaknesses were:

- Time-consuming update of concordance which is substantially rebuilt overnight to incorporate changes made during the day.
- Difficulty of integration with other software. CALL IN is not supported and CALL OUT is available only with the assistance of the suppliers. It is not easy to use external editors.
- The lack of a UNIX version.
- Word positions are not held in the inverted files. Proximity searching is made sequentially on an initial result stack.

INFO-TEXT Here the suppliers did not respond to our repeated requests for information.

MIMER-IR Not investigated in depth because of the fact that it is really a supplementary product to their relational offering.

SUPERFILE Available only under Unix and VMS, has no proximity searching facility, no on-line help facility, no built-in thesaurus and according to its suppliers could not handle the Shakespeare or Homer data sets.

Bibliography

[1] Anon. Bringing the free-text explosion under control. *Dec User*, (January):42–44, 1988.

[2] J. Ashford. Information storage and retrieval systems on mainframes and minicomputers: a comparison of text retrieval packages available in the uk. *Program*, 18:124–146, 1984.

[3] J.H. Ashford. Storage and retrieval of bibliographic records: comparison of database management system (dbms) and free text approaches. *Program*, 18:16–45, 1984.

[4] J.H. Ashford and D. Matkin. *Studies In The Application Of Free Text Package Systems*. Library Association, London, 1982.

[5] W.B. Croft. An overview of information systems. *Information Technology: Research and Development*, 1:73–96, 1982.

[6] H. Dyer and A. Brookes. *A Directory Of Library And Information Retrieval Software For Microcomputers*. Gower, Aldershot, 1986.

[7] B. Gerrie. *Online Information Systems. Use And Operating Characteristics, Limitations And Design Alternatives*. Information Resources Press, Arlington, Va., 1983.

[8] N. Goldsmith. An appraisal of factors affecting the performance of text retrieval systems. *Information Technology: Research and Development*, 1:41–53, 1982.

[9] P.O'N. Hoey. Comparison of CAIRS and STATUS information storage and retrieval software over a 3-month period. *Information Processing and Management*, 18:117–123, 1982.

[10] J.J. Hughes. Text retrieval programs - a brief introduction. *Bits &
     Bytes Review*, 1:1–5, 1987.

[11] J.H.Ashford and P.Willett. *Text Retrieval and Document Databases*.
     Chartwell Bratt, London, 1988.

[12] M.E.D. Koenig. Data relationships: bibliographic information
     retrieval systems and database systems. *Information Technology and
     Libraries*, 4:247–272, 1985.

[13] I.A. Macleod and R.G. Crawford. Document retrieval as a database
     application. *Information Technology: Research and Development*,
     2:43–60, 1983.

[14] J. Minker. Information storage and retrieval - a survey and
     functional description. *ACM SIGIR Forum*, 12:1–108, 1977.

[15] editor R. Kimberley. *Text Retrieval: A Directory Of Software. 2nd
     Edition*. Gower, Aldershot, 1986.

[16] J.E. Rowley. An overview of microcomputer text retrieval packages.
     Aslib Proceedings, 40:311–319, 1988.

[17] G. Salton. *Automatic Text Processing: The transformation, analysis
     and retrieval of information by computer*. Addison-Wesley, Reading
     MA., 1989.

[18] G. Salton and M.J. McGill. *Introduction To Modern Information
     Retrieval*. McGraw-Hill, New York, 1983.

[19] M.E. Williams. Electronic databases. *Science*, 228:445–456, 1985.